GW00648972

Huge thanks and love to Rachel Catherall – my partner, best friend and general crazy loon

Dedicated to the memory of my mate, Jon Hall, who was taken away from us far too early

Contents

ABOUT THIS BOOK

Welcome to this user-friendly guide to putting on a dance school / studio show in a professional venue from a technical perspective. It can be a pretty stressful task, there is so much you are assumed to know, so much you think you should know, so much you think you do know, yet often, there is no resource covering all aspects to help and answer your questions. This is where this guide comes in. Hopefully this book will take off some of the stress and give you an idea of ways you can make the whole experience a lot more pleasurable and give you a better understanding of some of the technical jargon that puts the fear into many. Even if you have been putting on shows for years, I'm sure you will still find the information in this book invaluable. It will probably cover a lot of things you already know, but I promise there will be a lot in here that you have never even thought of, and that extra information could lead to a much more pleasant experience, and possibly help you save money too.

The book is split into bite sized chunks and can be read in or out of order, depending on your knowledge of the subject. I have purposely kept it simple, but explaining any technical terms in just as much detail as you need to know along the way.

By the end of this book, you will have a better insight in all things technical associated with a production. How lighting works in your show and what is realistically achievable with the available equipment. How to best compile your sound and learn about basic sound editing. If using video in your show, you will learn what you are able to achieve relatively easily and also what is more complicated. All that, and much more, including stage terminology, stage geography and learning how to, 'call a show'.

In addition to the technical information in the book, there are sections regarding Copyright, Child Licensing, Theatre Etiquette, Hints & Tips and much more.

By purchasing this book, you will have free access to exclusive online content featuring videos and useful downloads covered in the book. There is a section at the end of this book explaining how to access this content.

ABOUT THE AUTHOR

Matthew Williams, known to everyone as Wills, trained at Clwyd Theatr Cymru (formerly Theatr Clwyd and now back to being called Theatr Clwyd again) and at the School of Sound Recording, Manchester.

Currently in charge of all things Sound & AV (Audio Visual) at Theatr Clwyd, Wills has been sound designer for over 80 Theatr Clwyd / Clwyd Theatr Cymru productions over the last 26 years or so, taking him all round Wales, parts of the UK, including London, plus a show in New York, as well as designing sound for other production companies, including a production of, 'Ghosts' in a theatre in Seattle. A sound design for a new musical in London in 2016 earned him a nomination for a Best Sound Design Award.

Wills' sound designs have been featured in exhibitions in various places, including, online, multiple venues in the UK, the V&A Museum in London and at an arts festival in Taipei.

He met his partner, Rachel over 20 years ago at the theatre. A then professional dancer, now turned choreographer, who was directing her mother's dance school show at the venue. A few years later, Rachel took over the running of the school and it has grown to become one of the most successful dance schools in North Wales. Wills is a partner in the business and deals with most of the technical requirements for shows and events.

Back in the late 90's, Wills, along with friends, Jon Hall and 'Wes' Groom, started up a recording services company called, 'Merlin Music' that specialised in recording packages for male voice choirs. Later, Wills and Jon went on to form an independent record label called, 'Spank Records' and worked with many established bands.

Since 1997, Wills has had a great working relationship with Tyla J. Pallas - the lead singer of UK rock band, The Dogs D'Amour. To date, Wills has been involved in one way or another, either engineering, mastering, editing or DVD authoring over 30 releases by Tyla on his label, King Outlaw Records.

Other independent record labels that Wills has been involved in their releases include, Changes One Records, Stone Me Records, Provocateur Records, Desert Inn Records and also cast recordings from shows produced by Clwyd Theatr Cymru.

Wills also runs an audio services company called, 'WW Audio' which offers sound editing, sound effect libraries and educational services.

At the time of writing, he has released 9 sound effects libraries and 3 field recording albums under the name of WW Audio. He has also released 3 sound art albums under his artist name, 'Caliginous'.

For more info and a full biography & CV, visit wwaudio.co.uk

INTRODUCTION

It's coming up to that time of year, time for your annual dance show. Maybe you're new to this and it's your first time, maybe you have been doing it for years, or maybe you are switching venue for the first time in a while. Whatever your situation, there are a number of options when hiring a venue.

Depending on what you want and maybe more importantly, what is available, you may be faced with a number of options. The three listed below are probably going to be the most common that you come across.

Dry Hire - You may just want to hire a space, such as a function room, school hall, or community centre, that although may have some basic lighting and sound facilities, they may not provide any operators or staff. The only staff member you may come across in this situation is maybe a care taker, someone who has to be there for insurance purposes while you are in the building, who is responsible for locking up at the end of the night. If this is the case you will need to find out what facilities are available and provide your own people to operate.

Small Scale Venue - It may be that the venue you hire has a small theatre type set up with decent, but basic facilities and they provide a single technician. This is great and a very common option, but be aware that if the single technician is responsible for the lighting, the sound and all other technical elements of your show, there in only so much that one person can do in the time provided. In this situation, with consultation with the venue, if you could provide some additional skilled people, it could take some pressure of the technician. Although not always the case, both this type of hire and the dry hire will usually be for a set hire cost, and will have various conditions attached.

Large Theatre - If you hire a larger theatre, you may have the luxury of a full technical team. This may include a lighting operator, sound operator, stage crew and fly person. This may sound ideal, but the more people you use from the venue, the more it will ultimately cost you. You need to decide what is important for your production and what it is you are actually trying to achieve. In this type of situation, it may be that rather than a hire fee, you actually work on a percentage split of sales with the venue, often with additional costs on top of that.

It's worth pointing out, that there is no right way or wrong way to put on a show, but there are certain procedures that are common place and some that maybe you hadn't thought of, that would make your production run a lot smoother, with possibly better results and ultimately, could help save you some money. This book takes my experience of working on more dance shows than I could ever dare to remember over the last 26 years or so, and passing on my observations and knowledge to help you have a better time, in what is often a stressful experience.

YOU'VE FOUND A VENUE, WHAT NEXT?

So, you have found a venue that suits your needs, you know what type of hire you need and have spoken with the person who takes the bookings to see if it is available when you want it, and you're looking to confirm and get a contract with them.

It could be that this is done over the phone or via email, but it certainly makes sense, especially if it's a venue that you haven't used before, to arrange to meet them and have a look around to double check it suits your needs. There are a number of questions that you need to be asking.

There are also some technical questions that you should be asking, that maybe only the technician working on your show will be able to answer, if that is the case, try and organise a meeting with them too.

The next section concentrates on a number of questions that you should be thinking about, both before you book the venue and once you have booked. Between the person responsible for your booking and the technician from the venue (if you are using one), they should be able to give you the answers to most, if not all of these questions. There are also some subjects that you need to be aware of when producing a show that are also mentioned in the following section.

WHAT DO I NEED TO KNOW AND CONSIDER?

What type of hire is it for the venue? Is it a set fee, or a percentage split of sales?

How many hours and members of staff does the contract cover. What are the additional costs should you go over your agreed number of hours or require additional staff?

Make sure you are very clear on the times of your bookings. For example, if you are booked in a venue for a week for your show, and your booking states you have got the space for rehearsals from 5pm until 9pm, make sure you check if this takes in to account the arrival of the children into the building. Don't assume that people can arrive and be let into the venue before your allocated time. This is also similar for your fit up time. Be clear with exactly how much time you need and have available for each part of fit up process. By, 'Fit Up', I mean the period of time that you have to get the staging in place for your production, the lighting rigged and working, and all other technical equipment that needs installing for your show. This may also include time needed to get all of the costumes to the dressing rooms and maybe setting up signing in stations for the pupils. Always remember that anything you want to happen takes time to achieve, often a lot longer than you may think. If you want lots of staging or more than the standard lighting rig and if you require special effects, or maybe if you are using radio microphones, be aware that this all takes advanced planning and all takes up additional time. You can almost guarantee that any time taken up with your production will be charged back to you. For example, if your contract says that on your first rehearsal day, you have the venue booked from 9am - 5pm, that doesn't necessarily mean that the children can start rehearsing at 9am, time will always be needed to set up for the production, so always double check.

As well as considering the time it takes to get set up for your show, you also need to consider the time it takes to, 'get out' (or 'load out') your show. This is the time after the final show where you get everything that is yours out of the venue. Everything from staging, lighting, sound equipment, or absolutely anything that has been installed specifically for your production will usually have to come out after the final show, as the venue may be hosting another group or company the next day. Depending on the type of venue, your company type and the size of your set (if any), you may end up paying a premium rate, especially if it goes past midnight, so make sure you find out exactly what you will be charged beforehand, to avoid awkward questions after the event. It can be really useful to have a team of willing parents to help with the get out.

Are there any additional costs, such as a percentage of merchandise and programme sales if the theatre staff sell them for you?

Are there additional hire fees for the use of some equipment? Some venues have the option of moving lights, radio microphones, star cloths, projectors etc., but these often come at an additional cost.

What policies if any does the venue have with regards to signing children in and out of the building? Is it something they are happy to let the dance school deal with, or do they have a set procedure? To not comply with the venue's policy could be a breach of contract.

What documentation does the venue require from you? This may include insurance policies, risk assessments and proof of child licensing and licensed chaperones.

Does the venue deal with submitting the information to the PRS with regards to music licensing (there is a chapter going into more detail about this later in the book). If so, does the venue provide the relevant paperwork to be filled in, or is it up to the producer of the event (the dance school principal). You will usually find that if it's a dry hire or smaller venue, it will be the responsibility of the dance school to submit the music information to the PRS, where as a larger venue may just require you to fill in the forms and they submit the information.

What is the venue fire alarm procedure? Are they planning any scheduled fire alarm tests while you are there? It is best to find this out early on, as when you take your first rehearsal, or whenever there are different people from your group at the venue, you will need to inform everyone of what to do in the event of the fire alarm going off.

Are there enough dressing rooms for your pupils? Make sure you know in advance how many people the venue allows in each room, this will help when trying to organise who goes where. Some venues may offer to make some additional changing spaces, maybe offstage or in rooms that are not traditionally used by the venue as dressing rooms. In schools, the dressing rooms are often class rooms, so make sure you check what you can or cannot take in there. There may be, 'no food backstage' policies etc. You may need to know how many power sockets there are in there and how much you can safely plug into them. It is also worth checking what type of fire sensing system they have in the rooms. Depending on the type of sensor, some systems can be set off by hair spray and on some occasions, by a camera flash. Make sure you check to see if there are any known issues like this to avoid embarrassment and potential cost when you hire the space.

Does the venue have a show relay or calls system backstage to enable people in the dressing rooms to hear the show and receive their calls to the stage? If not, you will need to think about getting a team of runners to make sure the correct children are at the stage at the right time.
If for example, your shows are split over a number of weekends, check if it possible to store your equipment, costumes etc. at the venue during the week days, or does everything have to be taken out after the first weekend and taken back in the following weekend?

Do you want to film your show? As part of the Child Protection Licence conditions, you need to get permission from all of the parents and guardians of the children if you are filming the show. A good way to avoid the hassle of getting permission every time, is including that you intend to film all performances and have photographs taken, as part of your dance school or studio policy, with an opt out if people aren't happy. If you are having the show filmed, either doing it yourself or getting a company in to do it for you, make sure you check with the venue that they allow this. There should be no reason for them to not allow you, providing you have gone through the correct procedures within your school / studio, but from experience, some venues can have a policy of no filming, regardless of if it's your company and even if you have consent from all of the parents and guardians of the children.

Assuming it is ok with the venue, it is worth organising early on where the camera or cameras will be situated. It may be that seats need to be taken out, or at least taken off sale. You may need to check if there is a power outlet for the cameras as you may not be able to run power extension cables along the auditorium. It may be that whoever is filming will require an audio feed of the show from the sound mixing desk. Make sure you check if this is possible, rather than just turning up on the day and expecting it. If it is possible, it's worth checking with the person who will be operating the camera, what type of connector is needed from the sound desk to plug into their camera. Some cameras take a 3 pin cannon connector called an, 'XLR', and some may require a, '1/4 inch jack'. If you could get this information to the sound operator prior to the camera operator turning up, they can think about it when setting up the sound desk for your show and can save a lot of time.

Are there any quick-change areas? Similar to the dressing room, the quick-change area is often a custom-made space, usually made up of theatre staging flattage (large, usually canvas covered rectangular frames), off the side of the stage, for the occasions where there isn't time for the dancer to get back to their dressing room (which could potentially be elsewhere in the building). Check with the production technician of the venue if this is something that might be available to you, and if so, where they are situated.

It is also useful to ask if there can be a light in there and maybe a mirror too. Forward thinking of this can save a lot of time when you start rehearsals.

Ask about the venue's chaperone policy. Although it has been the law for many years about who can or cannot look after children backstage, many venues have been fairly relaxed about it and have assumed the dance school are carrying out the correct procedures, which often wasn't the case. Venues are now becoming a lot stricter on correct procedure of child protection. A parent can only look after their own child, which isn't really useful for a dance school show, so depending on the number of children aged 16 (if they are still in full time education) or under in the production, you need a certain amount of registered chaperone / matron licence holders. Using parents who are just police checked is not acceptable. Bear in mind, that it costs, and can take a few months to obtain a chaperone / matron licence, so make sure if you need to do this for your show, that you allow plenty of time, or you may end up having to hire in licensed chaperones especially for your production. In the UK, by law, any child in and up to secondary education, even if they are 16, has to be chaperoned at all times. This includes toilet visits and even meeting parents at stage door to receive food /

belongings etc. To apply for a chaperone / matron license, you have to apply through your local council. There is a section dedicated to chaperones later in the book.

Make sure you understand the child licensing policy with regards to performances. There is a more detailed section about child licensing later in this book, but I'll touch briefly on it now. Although it should be fairly straight forward, child licensing still causes a lot of confusion, with both venues and dance schools. There is a lot of information online regarding this, but there are inconsistencies and slightly different interpretations, especially from county to county. Basically, if a child (up to and including 16 if still in full time education) is performing in a production that isn't part of their regular school education and the production has a paying audience, then the county has to be informed. If that child is only performing up to four times within a six-month period then a child performance licence isn't required and the child is exempt. This is where it gets confusing. Many people think that if this is the case, then nothing more needs to be done, but that isn't quite correct. Even if a child is exempt from needing a performance licence, details of the child still need to be submitted to the child licensing department to obtain an, 'Exemption Certificate'.

Both exemption certificates and child performance licences require quite a lot of information submitting from both parents and teachers. Many counties will allow dance groups and performance groups who perform on a regular basis to apply for what is called a, 'Body of Persons Approval' licence. This makes life a little easier on the group as once granted, although the authorities still need to be informed of every child performing each time they are in a production or competition etc., there isn't the additional paperwork that is involved in an application for a normal Child Performance Licence including parent's and teacher's signatures. If in any doubt, always check with your local authority.

This is also a good time to talk about the sort of lighting you want for the show. If it wants to be fairly generic, or if you want certain things at certain times, ask to see what is available. If you want additional equipment related to lighting, such as star cloths, mirror balls etc. the meeting is a good time to discuss all of that in case additional equipment needs to be sourced or hired from elsewhere. There is a chapter later on discussing lighting in more detail.

Make sure you check what format the venue requires your sound to be given to them. It may be that some venues require compact discs, maybe mini disc, some may want all of the music as audio files given to them on a USB drive, or maybe they require the music to be emailed in advance. Also, talk about what microphones you may need. How many radio mics, if any you would like, and if so, what type of radio mic? See what is and isn't available to you. There is a whole section covering sound and microphones in a later chapter.

If you're planning on using video projection in your production, check with the technician what is or isn't available to you. There is a section covering video projection later in the book.

If you would like to use pyrotechnics in your show, again, check what is available and also what is allowed and if there are any types of pyrotechnic that the venue doesn't allow. These are all things in advance that both yourself and the venue need to give a bit of thought about prior to you turning up on your first day. Again, there are sections covering pyrotechnics and other special effects later on in the book.

WHO DO I NEED & WHAT DO THEY DO?

We're now all happy that we have booked the venue. We have asked all of the questions we think we need the answers to, but if you've put on shows before, you'll know what a big operation it is and you know that you can't do it by yourself.

So, who do we need, and what do they do? Below is a list of jobs of people who could potentially be involved in your production. It may be that the scale of your show doesn't need all of these people, but this is based on a larger scale production. It is worth noting that, although some of these jobs may have to be done by the venue technicians, many of them can be done by helpful parents, or more commonly, past pupils, or pupils who for some reason can't be in the show.

Director - This is often the dance studio / school owner, or at least the person responsible for creating the production. Although they may not have choreographed every routine, it is useful to have a person responsible for taking all of the routines and turning it into a show.

Stage Manager - The person who takes responsibility of everything that happens on the stage.

Show Caller - This is someone who is responsible for running the show, for giving the lighting and sound cues and any other cues needed for the show. There is a whole section dedicated to this later on in the book.

Wardrobe - It can be really useful to have a wardrobe person or team, people who can adjust or maintain costumes during the duration of the rehearsal period and the show.

Head Chaperone / Chaperones - To put on a show of any kind with a paying audience, it is a legal requirement that you have a number of registered chaperones looking after anybody under the school leaving age. The number of chaperones depends on the number of children. There is a section towards the end of the book which goes into a lot more detail about chaperones. From experience, it seems to help if there is a Head Chaperone, who is responsible for coordinating the other chaperones.

Stage Crew - These are people who help the stage manager and help doing any jobs on stage prior to, and during the production. This can include anything from sweeping the stage to putting bits of set on and off the stage.

Lighting Operator - This is the person who controls the lighting for your show. The operator may also be the lighting designer, the person responsible for creating the lighting states for your show.

Sound Operator - This is the person who controls the sound for your show. They play the music and mix the levels of the microphones.

Sound Number 2 - This is the person who looks after and deals with the radio microphones on the stage. There is a section explaining in detail later in the book about the role of the Sound Number 2.

Follow Spot Operator - This is the person who controls the follow spot (moving spotlight that follows the performer around on the stage).

Runners - These are people who are on hand to go to dressing rooms to collect the right people at the right time for the show.

Fly Person - If you are using any sort of scenery that 'flies in' or 'flies out', or if you are using, 'house tabs', then this is the person who does that. There is more about this later in the book.

Programme Sellers - If you're selling programmes, often a professional venue will charge you a commission if their staff sell them for you, so it may be worth providing some people to sell them yourself.

Registration Desk / Security - Regardless of the size of the venue, it can be useful to have somebody, or a few people who are responsible for signing in and out all of the children (along with the chaperones) and who are situated at all entrances and exits to make sure no child goes out of the area that they are meant to be in, but also to make sure no one goes into their area who shouldn't be there.

STAGING

Does your production require anything else other than a bare, flat stage, with no dressing apart from maybe some lights? If not, great, but if you do, depending on the size of the venue, they may be able to provide various different types of staging options. Don't take this for granted though, as many smaller venues may not have any facilities other than a standard bare stage, a general lighting rig and a basic sound system.

Does your show require dance floor? By, 'Dance Floor', I mean the professional vinyl type covering that is rolled onto a stage to provide a safe and often better than just bare surface to dance on. If required, check with the venue if this is an option. Some venues will have dance floor laid down by default for your show, but you may need to request it in some venues if you would like it.

One thing to bear in mind is, if your show has a lot of tap dance in it, vinyl dance floor can often reduce the sound greatly of the taps, a lot more so than if they were dancing on just a wooden stage. It is though possible, if the equipment is available, for the floor to have a number of microphones to pick up the tap sound, but don't assume that this will be an option. It may be that the actual stage flooring isn't suitable for dancing on, especially if there is any dancing in bare feet or socks, so a dance floor covering may be the only option. It's good just to be aware of this and bare it in mind when planning your show.

Getting back to, 'staging', the most common is in the form of rostrum (or rostra for plural). This is a raised platform, made of a single, or a number of individual platforms to provide different levels to perform on. A common type of rostrum is, 'Steel Deck'. Although steel deck is a fairly generic term for staging, it is actually a company brand name rather than a generic product name, just like Hoover has become a name often used for vacuum cleaners. A steel deck (I will use the term generically), is a heavy steel frame, with a wooden board on top. The most common sizes are 8ft long by 4ft wide, and can be used individually or bolted together to form a solid staging platform to perform on. They do come in other sizes, but the 8ft by 4ft are the most common. You can sit these decks directly onto the floor, or you can insert scaffolding poles (legs) into the corners to raise the height of them.

Bear in mind that once raised off the floor, depending on the height, or the venue's rules, hand rails may need to be attached to them along one or more of the edges as a safety barrier.

There are some examples of different steel deck and staging configurations in the videos on the website (more information about this at the end of this book).

If your production is of a larger scale and budget, and is maybe more of a production show rather than just a straight dance show, you may want to consider using an actual theatre set to dress your stage. You only need to do an online search for theatre set hire companies near you. In the UK, there are lots of companies that hire stage sets, such as, Scenic (www.scenicprojects.co.uk), Proscenium (www.prosceneium.co.uk), UK Productions (www.ukproductions.co.uk), Stage A Show (www.stageashow.org), amongst others, that can provide complete or partial sets, usually themed for musical theatre shows or pantomimes. If budget allows and if it's right for the production, this can be a great way to create a different look and feel to your show, and to make the stage look a lot more professional, but like everything else, it comes at a cost. It can cost thousands of pounds to hire a set for a week and have it delivered and picked up (usually on an articulated lorry). If you were looking into hiring a set for the week, from experience, you would probably be looking at somewhere between £2000 and £5000 including delivery and pick up. You also need to take into account the size of the set compared to the size of the venue. Many stages just won't be big enough, either onstage or offstage, where as other stages may be bigger than the actual set is designed for, so if you are hiring a set, always check with the venue for the stage area's dimensions first. In addition to that, you need to take into account the extra time and people it will take to put the set up and take it back down again at the end of the run of shows, all at a cost.

There are various other ways you can dress the stage that cost a lot less money, such as home built sets, or even using domestic items like tall standard household lamps, crates, cases, rugs, anything really, providing that it is useful for your show and that the venue are happy to have it on their stage.

If you bring anything electrical into the venue, there is a very strong chance that they will insist on it being, 'PAT Tested' (Portable Appliance Test) to make sure it is electrically safe to be used. You may need to show proof in the form of a test certificate to show that it has been tested. Some larger venues may be able to do this for you, or if not, they may be able to advise you as to where you can get it done.

Anything you want to bring onto the stage will need to be flame proofed. You can use a product called, 'Flambar' to spray over any items. You can get it easily online in 1 litre spray bottles for around £15 or so, or in 5 litre bottles for around £35.

An inexpensive but effective way to give the stage a different look is to hang lengths of material from the flying bars (see next section). These can instantly change the appearance of a stage, and depending on the colour of them, they can maybe be creatively lit by the stage lighting or even projected onto. Check out the video on the website to see an example of this. Don't forget, these will need to be flame proofed before you put them up.

You can be as creative or as simple as you want (time and budget depending of course), there are no rules as long as it's safe. Although, in my experience, the majority of dance shows are performed either on a flat stage or with a raised row of steel deck of the back of the stage.

USEFUL STAGE & BACKSTAGE THEATRE TERMINOLOGY

Before we move onto lighting and sound, I thought it would be useful to explain a bit about some of the terminology and names that are given to various things both on stage and off stage. These are words or phrases used in professional theatre, or by venue staff. If you don't know what they are talking about, it could be a little intimidating or just confusing, but getting familiar with certain terms will not only help you understand what is being talked about, but it will allow you to more accurately describe things to the technicians.

Proscenium Arch - The proscenium arch or, pros, as it is usually referred to, is the surrounding frame separating the stage from the auditorium. It is usually at the most downstage point of the stage.

Orchestra Pit - Many traditional theatres have an orchestra pit. It is a low level pit, lower than the floor of the auditorium, downstage (see Theatre Geography section later in the book) of the proscenium arch, where an orchestra would traditionally be during a musical performance.

Pit Lifts - If the venue has an orchestra pit, there is a good chance that they have pit lifts. This is basically the floor of the orchestra pit on top of motors, when not needed as an orchestra pit, can be lifted up to stage level to create an extension of the stage where the orchestra pit was, to create an apron.

Apron - This is the area of the stage downstage of (in front from the perspective of looking from the stage into the audience) the pros where traditionally an orchestra pit may be.

Passerelle - This is a walkway or boardwalk, or even just a continuation of the stage around the orchestra pit, allowing you to walk all the way around it at stage level.

Flying Bars and Flying - Flying bars are the long bars that run across the width of some stages that theatre lighting and scenery are hung on. Flying is the term for the bars being brought in and out (up and down). This is either done by a motor and a controller or by the 'Fly Man', or 'Fly Person', physically pulling on a rope as part of a counterweighted system. When a bar is pulled down towards the stage, it is known as 'flying in', when it's going up away from the stage, it's known as, 'flying out'.

House Tabs - Also known as just, 'tabs', are the usually heavy curtains on the front of the stage, near the 'pros', to hide the set as the audience come into the auditorium. Some shows start with the tabs in to hide any set dressing they may have, or some may start without any at all, revealing the stage as the audience enter. They are also often used at the interval and at the end during the curtain call (bows). There is no rule on if you should use house tabs or not, it is purely personal preference.

Iron / Safety Curtain - Also known as the, 'fire curtain', this is a large, metal wall like structure that flies in, usually butted up to the pros that acts as a barrier to stop a fire on stage from spreading into the auditorium or a fire in the auditorium from spreading to the stage. Not all venues have a safety curtain, but if they do, it is a legal requirement for it to be shown to be working when a number of audience members are in the auditorium. The iron is traditionally brought in during the interval.

Travellers - These are usually 2 stage curtains, often black, on a track with a rope on one end to pull, to allow you to open and close them. They can be fitted to any of the flying bars enabling you to section off parts of the stage. If it's a smaller venue that doesn't have flying bars, very often, their front stage curtain, or house tabs work in the same way as travellers, allowing the curtains to be opened and closed by the pulling of a rope (or motorised).

Full Blacks - In a similar way to how travellers can be used to section off part of the stage, so can a full black. This is generally a large black cloth that can be flown in (see previous) to section off a part of the stage. Unlike the travellers which open and close, this just flies in and flies out.

Staging Rostrum / Rostra - We mentioned this earlier, but just to go over again, this the name given to modular staging pieces. They come in different shapes, sizes and materials. A common form of rostra is, 'Steel Deck', which although is a brand name, it has become the commonly used name for this type of staging. This is a metal frame, with a wooden top. They come in different sizes, but the most common is 8 ft by 4 ft, with half pieces being 4 ft by 4 ft. These can be built and bolted together to form bigger structures. A single deck is referred to as a rostrum, whereas the plural is rostra.

Treads - These are most commonly wooden step sections that are used as access to the rostrum or the stage.

Dance Floor - Also mentioned earlier, this is the name for the vinyl strips of flooring that are rolled out on the stage and taped together to form the surface of the dance area. This provides a slightly cushioned and often better surface for the dancer to dance on, rather than just on a wooden stage.

Cans / Comms - This is the name given to the headphones and communication system used by all of the operators, stage crew etc. This usually consists of a box which can clip onto your belt, with a pair of headphones, with an attached microphone plugged into it. They usually have a button that you push to enable the microphone so you can talk to others wearing the cans, and they have a volume control, which controls the level of how loud you hear everyone else. Both terms, cans and comms are commonly used. Cans is a traditional name for headphones and comms is short for communications. There is no right or wrong, and any venue technician will know what you are talking about regardless of which word you use.

Cue Lights - Although not really common in dance shows, more so for actual productions, a cue light is usually a small box with 2 lights attached, a red and a green light. These are controlled by the person who is cueing or calling (running) the show and are used to show the performer when they need to enter the stage. Similar to a traffic light system, when the red light is lit, the performer knows that they should be getting ready to go onto the stage, when the green light is lit, that is their cue to enter onto the stage.

Calls - The person calling the show will almost always have some sort of microphone / communication system to allow them to give messages to backstage relay speakers. The speakers are often positioned in dressing rooms or corridors and allow calls to be made for certain people or groups of people to be given information or instructions, such as letting people know it's time for them to make their way to the stage. You will often hear relay speakers referred to as, 'Tannoy' speakers. Tannoy is a name of a company who produce loudspeakers and in a similar way to Steeldeck having become a generic name for staging rostrum, Tannoy is often used as a generic name for relay speakers.

Show Relay - Many venues (not all) will have some sort of show relay system installed. This is basically a system consisting of a microphone placed somewhere in the auditorium or maybe above stage, that enables people backstage or in dressing rooms to hear what is going on from the stage from wall mounted speakers.

LIGHTING

Lighting can play huge part in your production if you want it to. To get a good lighting designer / operator onboard will make a huge difference to how your show looks and is perceived. Yes, the show may primarily be about the dance routines, but don't forget, that is only part of the overall picture. Many dance schools that I have worked with over the years just turn up and say, 'I don't care what the lighting is like, just make sure that it's bright and you can see their faces'. This is all well and good if you're not bothered about the overall look of your show, but remember, at the end of the day, this is your shop window, so if time and budget allows, why not put in that extra bit of effort to make something a bit more special, not only for the audience, but for the performers, who have probably been rehearsing for months and this may be one of their only times on a professional stage.

It may be that you want to have more of an input into the lighting of your show, but don't know what is achievable or what terminology to use. This chapter should help give you a better understanding of the process.

If you are lucky, the venue may have a good and experienced lighting operator, who is quick and can make the show look great without much input from you, but remember, they don't know your piece like you do, they may only see it once in a rehearsal, or sometimes not at all, so from experience, I would say that most lighting operators would appreciate a bit of input from you, even if it's only a list of the costume colours for each number and maybe a short description of the routine. For example, you probably wouldn't want a nice, bright, multicoloured lighting state if you were performing Michael Jackson's Thriller. You may want it dark, smoky and spooky. Don't assume that the lighting operator knows the piece of music or style just from the title. One important thing to remember is, try not to be intimidated by the technology. Dancing is your world, theatre is the technician's world, you may occasionally come across a technician who doesn't like being told what to do, or may have the attitude of, "that is what I have made for you, that's all you're getting.". It's not a very useful attitude, and always remember, you're paying them to provide you with a service, not the other way around. Saying that, there has to be an understanding of what is achievable with the resources and time available. A lack of this knowledge may end up costing you time and ultimately, money.

Later in this chapter are some examples of how to submit information to the lighting operator and also examples of some lighting cue sheets. There are also examples of lighting styles on the videos on the website.

PLUGGING IN AND CONTROLLING THE LIGHTING

Even though there is no real need for you to understand how the plugging in and controlling of the lighting works, as this is the job of the technician, I thought it might be useful to have a basic understanding of what is involved.

The operation of plugging up and controlling a lantern is quite straight forward. The lantern is plugged into a socket which is numbered. This is usually referred to as a circuit. Each socket, or circuit in the venue is connected to it's own control dimmer, similar to the ones you may have at home that let you dim your lighting from nothing (0%) to full brightness (100%). There is a dimmer for every circuit in the venue, and they are usually in the form of, 'Dimmer Racks' which are just units containing multiple dimmers, each with their own fuse or trip switch. In larger venues, the dimmer racks are often in a different room away from the stage, in smaller venues, they might be attached to the wall at the side of the stage.

Within the lighting desk, the circuit number that you plugged your lantern into is assigned a, 'Channel Number'. This channel number is the number that the lighting desk uses to control that individual lantern that you plugged in.

For example, if there were 125 circuits covering the area of the stage and you had plugged your lantern into circuit number 85 (which is connected to dimmer number 85), but for convenience, you wanted to identify that lantern as number 1. Within the lighting desk, you would program, or, 'patch' the desk so that when you turned on channel 1, it turned on the lantern that was plugged into circuit 85.

There is no reason why the circuit number and the channel number can't have the same number, so the lantern plugged into circuit 10 is controlled by channel 10, but it is often not done that way for convenience. When the channel and the dimmer / circuit are the same number, it is known as a, '1 to 1 Patch'.

Let's say for example that you have a row of 5 lanterns on a flying bar that are plugged into circuits 50 - 54, you have another row of 5 lanterns on a flying bar further downstage that are plugged into circuits 25 - 29, and another row of 5 lanterns plugged into circuits 7 - 11. There is no reason at all why when controlling them from the lighting desk, you couldn't use the same numbers as the circuits, but if they are lanterns that you often want to use together in a group, rather than typing into the desk, 7 - 11, 25 - 29, 50 - 54, you could just assign them to channel numbers 1 - 15. There is no right or wrong, it is just done for convenience.

There are slight variations to this and moving lights work in a slightly different way, but essentially, that's how it works for most of the situations you are likely to be in.

LIGHTING TERMINOLOGY

This book isn't a guide to stage lighting, sound or theatre craft in general, but it will explain a few basic points that will help you understand a little bit of the technical world, which ultimately will help you understand what is and what may not be realistic. Below is a list of some of the basic names and terminology related to lighting, from a technician's perspective. Do be aware that some terminology can be different, depending on the country you are in. These are from a British perspective, but many are worldwide terms.

LX - This is short for, 'Electrics', but is also the generic name given to lighting. So, you would have an LX operator, which is the person operating the lighting and you would have LX Cues which refer to the lighting states for the production. If you are writing down the lighting cues, you would short hand it to LX Q, followed by the number that the lighting state is recorded as in the lighting desk.

Lighting Console / Desk - This is the (often) computerised control for programming, recording and recalling lighting states. In their most simple form, they will have a number of faders, each one controlling individual lanterns that you can push up or down to fade up or fade down the light. In it's most complex form, it is a high-powered computer that requires specialist programming knowledge.

Lantern - This is the name we give to an individual theatre light.

Moving Lights / Intelligent Lighting - Often referred to as, 'Movers', these are type of theatre lights that can be controlled from the lighting desk. They can usually move both up and down and left and right, often they can change colour and sometimes have their own built in gobos (see later). They allow more flexibility to the operator over a normal theatre lantern, which is often fixed and pointing to a single part of the stage in a single colour. Notice that I used the term, 'lights' rather than, 'lantern'. This is because, for some reason, although we refer to theatre lights as lanterns, for some reason, we still call moving lights, 'lights'.

Lighting Rig - A 'rig', is the term for the collection of lanterns or lights that have been put up for the production. These are usually hung on bars that fly in and out (up and down - see previous chapter), or are hung anywhere to enable the lighting designer / operator to light your show. Depending on your venue and budget, some spaces might have a, 'fixed rig', which means that the lights are in the same place for all productions that are in that venue, rather than custom made for your show, or there may be a bit of flexibility based on information you have given them. Within that, 'rig', there may be a combination of, 'generic' lighting, mixed with some moving or intelligent lighting (see above). The term, 'generic' in this case, just refers to a single fixed lantern pointing at a single, or particular spot on the stage (or where ever).

Do note, that to move or add a lantern within the rig might not be as simple as you think, in fact it can actually be quite a complex operation. Obviously each case is different, but it could be that to just add another lantern to the rig, it may take someone to, 'fly the bar in' (as mentioned, more about this later with explanations), if the theatre uses a counterweighted system for their lighting bars, it may require another person on another level of the stage to add some stage weights to counterbalance the bar for when the additional lantern is added, it then may require someone to run a cable from one part of the space, along the bar to the new lantern, the bar then has to, 'fly out'. Once the bar is up in the air, the lighting technician will then have to get access to the lantern, either by ladder, or maybe by some sort of access platform. They then need to point that lantern at the particular spot on the stage before it can be used. All that in itself, depending on the size of the venue could take two or even three people, ten minutes to do. Ten minutes just to put up one lantern - remember, you are paying for this time, so information in advance is always a good thing, for both you and the technician.

Lighting State - A lighting state is made up of a number of lanterns in the rig, being turned on to a particular level and then saved as a memory state on the lighting desk. It may be for one moment in a dance, you only want the lights on the upstage bar (see later chapter on stage geography) on at full brightness. The lighting operator would turn those particular lanterns on to 100% (full brightness) then save it on the lighting desk as a memory state. The next piece of lighting for the routine may want to add a spot light in the middle of the stage. The lighting operator then adds this spot light to the state and saves it again as another memory state. The whole show is built up by saving a number of memory states that can be recalled, usually in order, from the lighting desk. This is explained in a bit more detail in the next section.

Preset - This is usually a lighting state, often not cued by the person calling the show, that is on at the beginning as the audience come into the auditorium, before the show starts.

Post Set - This is usually a lighting state for the end of the show, post curtain calls, while the audience are leaving the auditorium.

Back Light - This is where the lanterns are upstage (towards the back), pointing downstage (towards the front), lighting the performer from behind.

Side Light - This is where the lanterns light the performer from the sides, this can be from lanterns on each end of the flying bars, also, often known as, 'Pipe Ends', or from lighting towers or booms on the side of stage.

Overhead Light - This is when the lanterns light the stage from overhead, often pointing straight down to create a general cover (see below) of light on the stage.

Front Light - This is light from the front of the stage, pointing at the front of the performer, often used to light faces.

Flood Light - A 'flood' is a term given to the type of beam a particular lantern produces and the job it is doing. Imagine it as a large, usually circular beam of light, when combined with others, covers large areas with an even brightness.

General Cover - This is a term relating to the large area of the stage being evenly lit using, 'flood' lights. An example may be that a rig has four rows of five flood lights, evenly spaced and focused (focused refers to the point in which a lantern is pointing at / focused to) at the stage, enabling an even, full cover of light on the stage.

Special - Opposite to general cover, a special is usually a single lantern pointing at a particular place, to highlight a particular thing (or person). For example, you could have a blue general cover on stage with a white special pointing to a particular point on stage which is lighting up a singer. Note that if you want to use specials in your show, make sure the lighting operator knows exactly where they need to be focused to. If it is a generic lantern that is being used as a special, it will require the lighting technician to physically get to the lantern and point it in the correct position on stage. If you change your mind afterwards, bear in mind that this can take time for the technician to get access to the lantern and physically point it to a different part of the stage, time of which you are paying for. If a moving light is being used for a special, then there is a bit more flexibility, as it can be controlled from the lighting desk, but remember the person or thing that is being lit by the special, needs to be in the same place in each performance. A really good tip is to train your dancers to tape marks during rehearsals. When rehearsing, if you mark out your floor in your rehearsal space with LX tape (electrical PVC tape) the same size, or a scaled size of the actual stage, then mark all of the special positions. Provided you put these in the same position when you get to the venue, your dancer will be trained to go to that position and a lantern can be focused to this spot and hopefully be constant every time.

Cyclorama or, 'Cyc' for short (pronounced, '*sike*') - Although not strictly to do with lighting as such, the 'cyc' is the large, usually white flat cloth that you often see at the back of the stage. The cyc is made from canvas or muslin and is one large piece of material, rather than one stitched together from smaller pieces. It will usually be stretched out, and the bottom weighted down to create a flat, plain surface which can then be lit or projected onto. Cyc's can be curved too, but in most instances, especially for dance, they are usually flat. The advantage of having a cyc for your dance piece is you can point particular lanterns at it to create large washes of colour or gobo effects (see below) to change the look and the feel of the stage.

Gobo - A 'gobo' is a thin, circular stencil or template, which is placed within a lantern, between it's lens and reflector, to create the image of the stenciled cut out in light on the surface it is pointed at. They are usually made out of a thin, tin like material, or occasionally glass. Gobos can be used to great advantage in your dance piece, creating patterns or shapes on the floor or cyc without the need for video projection. There are hundreds of different designs that you can get, or you can have them custom made to suit your needs. Many dance schools I have worked with over the years have their own custom-made gobo, with the name of their school or studio, which is then projected at the cyc or house tabs.

Smoke / Haze / Dry Ice - It is useful to understand the difference between various smoke effects. Smoke effects can have a dramatic effect of how the lighting looks on the stage and it is usually dealt with by the lighting technician and operated from the lighting desk. When we refer to, 'smoke' in this context, we usually mean that a blast of smoke is squirted from some form of smoke machine. These are usually in relatively short bursts and are for instant effect and usually disperses fairly quickly. Haze or Fog is something quite different to smoke. This is usually a constant (or at least for long durations) flow of fine mist like smoke which just lingers in the air. This can look stunning when caught in the beams of the light. If your routine requires the beams of light effects, you will almost certainly need some sort of haze or fog machine running to be able to create the effect. Dry ice is something quite different. Although a stunning effect, dry Ice isn't as common as you may think, due to the cost of the ice and the complexity of making it work correctly. This is a machine that melts frozen carbon dioxide blocks and creates the sort of long, lingering smoke that sits near the floor. It's the sort of thing you see in dodgy 80's music videos and large-scale shows, such as, Phantom of the Opera, when the boat is moving through the low smoke onstage. There are other types of smoke effects available, and take on many different forms, but the most common forms you will come across are smoke machines and hazers.

Lighting Gel / Colour Gel / Colour Filters - A gel is the coloured transparent material filter that is put in a 'colour frame' at the end of the lantern to make the beam a different colour. There are a number of different companies who produce this gel and hundreds of different shades of all colours. Most companies have a 'swatch book' which has small examples of each colour in their range. They are identified by the manufacturer's name or product range and an exclusive number for each shade of colour.

Follow Spot - This is the type of lantern that makes the large, circular beam of light that is used to follow a performer around the stage. It is usually a large lantern on a stand, that is often situated right at the back of the auditorium, in a control room, or it's own room, and requires an operator to physically move it and follow the performer on stage. Note that if you want to use a follow spot, if the venue allows, it would be worth your while providing an operator, as if you want the venue to provide one, you will end up paying for another member of staff doing a job that one of the student's parent's could maybe do. Interesting fact of the day alert - ABBA's song, 'Super Trouper' is about a follow spot, note the lyrics, 'Super Trouper lights are going to blind me'. Super Trouper is the brand name of a type of follow spot which was designed for use in arenas and large venues.

Ground Row - This is a type of lantern, often containing a number of lights, in different colours, which sits on the floor, and is often used to light up the cyc from below.

Lighting Boom / Side Lights - A lot of dance shows are not only lit from above, in front and from behind, but also from the sides. It is very common for there to be a number of poles or towers of some sort at the side of the stage, usually out of view from the audience, that have a number of lights pointing directly across the stage at different heights, usually shins, waste and head level. They are often referred to as, 'shins'. It is used to create another dimension of lighting. Just be aware though, that it reduces the space where the dancers go off from and they can potentially be walked or run into. There are many venues or technicians that won't use side lighting if there are younger children going to be onstage, just so they don't run into them.

Star Cloth - This is a large, usually black cloth, often hung at the back of the stage with small lights in it, creating a starry effect. They can differ in the fact that some are made with single colour pea lights, some with fibre optic, either single colour or changeable or more modern ones tend to be LED lights that are able to change colour and do various clever effects when controlled from the lighting desk.

Mirror Ball - Often referred to as a, 'Disco Ball', this is a ball shaped object, covered in many small mirrors. They are excellent for creating that classic disco effect. A light is shone at the mirror ball and the mirrors reflect the light around the space. Many of them have a small motor attachment to enable them to slowly spin.

Strobe - This is usually very bright flashes of white light in succession, creating almost like an old fashion movie effect. It is also good if trying to create thunder and lightning effects. Just be aware that the frequency (speed) of the strobing can affect people in different ways, especially people who are epileptic and can potentially cause seizures. If using a strobe effect, it's usually for no longer than a few seconds at a time. Most theatres will put up warning signs outside the auditorium, warning the audience that stroboscopic effects will be used in the production.

Chase Effect - This is an effect that is programmed from the lighting desk where one light turns on, followed by another, as the previous one goes out, followed by another etc. It is also known as a step effect. It's good for disco type lighting effects.

Silhouette - You can create a sort of silhouette effect on a performer if they are only lit from behind, so there is no light on the front of them at all. This can be really effective if a part of a routine wants to focus more on the shape of the performer, rather than the features.

Black Out - This is where all of the stage lighting is turned off. This would often happen at the end of a routine to show it's the end of the piece. It may be that you want a black out between routines for the dancers to get off stage and the new dancers to get on stage without being seen. Just be aware that some venues have a bit of a, 'health and safety' problem with this, and may insist on putting up a, 'Scene Change State" (see below).

Scene Change State - This is a lighting state with very low, usually dark blue lights which are on just enough for a performer to see to get off or on stage. Some venues or technicians insist on this, over a black out, especially if it's smaller children leaving and entering the stage. One compromise the venue may accept to having a black out, is if you have glow tape arrows where they need to exit stage and next to anything that could be run into, such as a lighting boom.

House Lights - These are the lights that light up the auditorium for the audience to see as they enter and leave the space. They are usually independent to the main lighting rig and are often controlled from the lighting desk, or sometimes controlled independently.

Tab Warmers - This is the name given to the light that is often lighting the front cloth, or house tabs whenever they are used. This is usually at the beginning of a show, the interval and the end. Similar to house lights, they are sometimes controlled from the lighting desk or can be controlled independently.

Blues - These are lights that light up the offstage areas so the performer can see when they get off stage. They are usually dark blue, so as not to bleed light onto the stage.

There are many other terms that are frequently used, but these are probably the most common. If you can get an understanding of these basic ones, it will help when communicating ideas with the technician.

LIGHTING YOUR SHOW

This section isn't a lesson in lighting design, as that is the job of the lighting designer / operator, but it's a simple insight of what is involved when someone lights your show. A little understanding of the process can help you firstly appreciate the time it takes to do certain tasks and also to help you get ideas and understand some of the potential of the rig in a little more detail.

A lighting designer will often start by making some, 'Groups'. This is where a number of lanterns are grouped together with control from the lighting desk, often by type, such as, back light, overhead light, side light, front light, general cover, and maybe by colour, and are often used as a starting point for each lighting state.

These groups of lanterns are, 'brought up' or turned on at varying percentage levels to build a 'lighting state'. Once the groups of lights have been brought up, the lighting designer may start to bring in individual lights or moving lights into the state.

Once they are happy with the look of the lighting state, they will record it as a scene memory or lighting memory state within the lighting desk, giving it a lighting cue number.

They will then build their next lighting state and record that as a memory state and give that another number. This continues until there is a lighting state or a number of lighting states for each routine or section of the show.

Once the lighting desk has all of the lighting states, or lighting cues, 'plotted' or saved into the desk, at the required time in the routine or at the end of the number etc. when given the command from the person calling the show (covered in a later section), it is as simple as the lighting operator pressing a button to cross to the next lighting cue.

So, for example, Lighting Cue 1, or LX Q1 as we would abbreviate it to, might be 20 different lanterns creating a 'general cover' over the whole stage in a particular colour, maybe consisting of lots of back light and side light, maybe a bit of overhead light and a little front light.

Maybe after the intro of the song, a singer comes onto stage and stands in the centre, the next lighting cue, or LX Q2 as we would call it, which may be to add a 'special' to light the singer as they get into position is then gone into.

Possibly during the instrumental section of the song, we want to take out the 'special' and bring up some different lights on a different part of the stage for the dancers We may want to change the colour of the cyc and back lights or side lights and possibly take out all of the front light. This could be recorded as LX Q3, and then maybe at the end, we want to go to a 'black out' (all of the lights out or at 0%), which could be LX Q4.

A routine can have as many lighting states as you want, it could be one, it could be one hundred. The only thing to bear in mind is, that each state has to be programmed into the lighting desk and therefore takes a certain amount of time. My advice, especially when working to a time and budget is to keep it simple but effective. Also, take advice from the technician, as this is their job, and they know about lighting, just as you know about dance.

There may be occasions where the lighting operator is, 'busking it' or making it up as they go along. It could be that they have already preprogrammed a number of basic groups and lighting states in different colours, covering different parts of the stage and are just fading or swapping from one to another during the routines. They might also have some states preprogrammed on, 'flash buttons' which are just buttons that you push to activate, then take your finger off to turn it off. It could be that on the flash buttons, they have some side lights programmed in, or maybe some single colour lights which they just flash on and off on top of the existing lighting state. There is no problem in this at all, it just means that it's not really customised to you and also may not be consistent over all of the performances. That's not to say this isn't a good way of doing it, with a creative operator, it could look amazing. There is no right or wrong way of doing it, it's just a matter of creativity, resources, time and budget.

TAPING THE STAGE

Taping the stage can be a very useful exercise and is something that many professional dance companies do to help with not just blocking the dancers on the stage, but also can be very useful for lighting.

It is common practice to put a small piece of PVC electrical tape, which can be bought in any DIY store, on to various points on the stage. These include the centre of the performance area, the centre at the front (the downstage centre edge of the dance floor) and also on the quarter point either side on the stage front.

This is an easy way for the dancer to get their bearings to where abouts on stage they are while under the bright theatre lighting. If while rehearsing in your studio or hall, you make a mockup of the stage with the tape on the floor, your dancers can be shown that they need to hit the certain marks for the routine. When they transfer to the venue, they will be used to hitting the marks and hopefully save a considerable amount of blocking time.

It is common practice for a line of tape to be put along the tab line of the stage (where the tabs come in at the end of the show). This is useful to show the dancers where they need to keep away from when the curtain is flying in.

The reason I have mentioned about taping the stage in this section is that using tape marks on the stage can help the person lighting your show.

For example, if you have a dancer that needs to be lit by a single special (see earlier chapter) and if there is a small tape mark, or, 'spike' as it is known as, then even without the dancer being there, the person lighting the show can focus the light to that position before they get there and as long as the dancer hits their mark, then the light will be pointing at them.

If you have any sort of props in your routine, for example, some chairs. If you 'spike' or mark where the legs of the chair are meant to be with a small piece of tape, then you know you can always find the exact position for them next time you put the chairs out and they will always be in the light.

If you have the luxury of having the time to sit with the lighting designer before your rehearsals, you could go through what you want in each number and work alongside them as they start to plot the lights for your show.

When lighting a show, it can be incredibly useful to have a 'walker'. This is someone who can stand on certain points on the stage during the lighting session, so the lighting designer can see the effect of the lights on a person in a certain position, rather than just a bare stage. Maybe use some of your students if they are available.

USING LIGHTING TO CREATE A LOOK OR EFFECTS

Remember that a lighting state doesn't have to be just a load of lights turned on brightly so you can see the dancer's faces, it can be used creatively to give a particular look to a routine in a similar way to staging.

Using smoke or haze with lighting can look really effective. The smoke is lit up by the beams of light and can add another dimension to your routine. This can be just basic shafts of light if using with generic lights, either with or without gobos, or you can add another dimension when used with moving lights.

Another common trick is to using lighting to create an appearing or disappearing effect when used with a gauze. In the way that a cyclorama is a large cloth that spans the stage, a gauze is similar, but is less dense, with small holes between the stitching. When you point a light at a gauze, it can look like a fairly solid piece of cloth, but when you add light from behind, it can make the area behind (upstage) appear and make the cloth look almost transparent. This is particularly good when trying to create a revealing type effect. For example, it could be a pantomime where the fairy is talking to the audience from the front of the stage and as they wave their magic wand, the magical world appears as if by magic behind them. There is an example of lighting through a gauze on the, 'Staging, Lighting & Effects Video 3' on the website. Using lighting to create shadows on the cyc is also another common trick. By pointing a light directly at someone in front of the cyc, it will create a shadow. You can use this creatively by adding more lights on different angles to create some very clever effects.

INFORMATION FOR THE LIGHTING DESIGNER

As mentioned earlier, it's really useful for the person responsible for lighting your show to have some information from you regarding each routine. They don't need essays worth of information, just the things that are important for them such as the song title, a brief description of the feel of the piece and costume colour information. Here is an example on how to set out that information easily. I have made a simple table, using a fictional name for a dance school and show. You can download this template from the website and modify it with your information.

Studio 97 - Dance Till You Drop - Lighting Notes

Number	Name	Description	Costumes	Feel
1	The Greatest Showman	Circus styled routine, full stage, no soloists	Mixture of red, silver, black	Up tempo, bright
2	Over the Rainbow	Solo singer and 2 dancers	Light blue for dancers, white for vocalist	Moody, dark, a special on the vocalist down stage right. Dark blues
3	Disco Inferno	Upbeat, disco feel, full stage, soloist near the end	Mixture of bright colours	Up tempo, bright, flashing disco feel. Soloist towards the end needs to be picked out, centre stage
4	Bye Bye Blackbird	Bob Fosse styled piece, 3 groups of dancers, 1 on each side of the stage and 1 in the centre	Black costumes, white gloves, lack hats	Mid-tempo, Light blue general cover with 3 pools of white light to cover the 3 group positions

This is generally enough information to make the lighting designer / operator happy to be getting on with. It may be that you have time scheduled to sit with them before, or during the rehearsal period to go through each number in more detail, maybe having a number of lighting state ideas for some of the routines, and being a bit more creative.

If you don't have the time to go through all your ideas with them, but you know the sort of thing that you want the lighting to do for you and what it might look like, you could be a bit more descriptive and make them a cue sheet. This doesn't have the information about costumes or the feel of the piece, but is a bit more detailed plan with regards to your lighting requirements.

In this example, there may be some terminology that you are not totally familiar with. This is all explained later in the book in the, 'Stage Geography' section.

The example shown, is a relatively simple styled cue sheet, showing how many lighting states or cues you want in the routine and what you want them to be doing or look like.

Always remember, the more complex it gets, the more time it takes. If you want the lighting to be more than just a basic, lighting state on at the beginning of the number and off at the end, make sure you allow the time for this to be programmed into the lighting desk.

This template is available to download from the website, to be edited as you need.

The videos section of the website has a number of examples of different types of lighting for dance shows. They may give you some inspiration on what can realistically be achieved with standard and specialised lighting equipment.

There is also a video that shows how to call, or cue the show, which relates to a chapter later on in the book.

Studio 97 - Dance Till You Drop - Lighting Cues

Routine	Name	LX Cue	Description
1	The Greatest Showman	LX Q1	Blackout on stage just before the house tabs fly out
		LX Q2	As the house tabs fly out, full stage, bright flashing lights
		LX Q3	Add white special, DSC as Barnum walks forward - approx 30 seconds into the track
		LX Q4	Take out white special as Barnum re-joins the group
		LX Q5	Blackout at the end of the number
2	Over the Rainbow	LX Q6	Full stage, light blue general cover
		LX Q7	Add white special to vocalist as she starts to sing, SR
		LX Q8	Take out white special on the instrumental break and make the general cover brighter
		LX Q9	Lower the general cover to original level and add in the white spot as vocalist sings again
		LX Q10	Fade to blackout over 5 seconds at the end of the song
3	Disco Inferno	LX Q11	Bright, flashing, reds and oranges. 1 lighting state all the way through
		LX Q12	Black out at end of the number
4	Bye Bye Blackbird	LX Q13	Dark blue general cover at the start
		LX Q14	Add a pool of white light, SR when the stage right group start moving
		LX Q15	Add a pool of white light, SL when the stage left group start moving
		LX Q16	Add a pool of white light, CS when the centre stage group start moving
		LX Q17	Take out all of the white pools of light when all 3 groups start to move together, lift the level of the dark blue general cover
		LX Q18	Blackout at the end of the routine

S O U N D

As with lighting, sound plays a huge part in your production. Bad quality audio tracks or bad microphone technique and operation can ruin the best of performances.

Over the last 20 years or so, sound technology has evolved at an incredible rate. When I started in theatre, back in the early 90's, we played sound for productions on 1/4-inch tape reel to reel machines. As time moved on, we went through cassette players, samplers, hard disk players, Minidisc, CD, but have now arrived firmly in the computer world.

Many dance schools and a large amount of festivals and competitions are keeping up with technology, many places will ask for your music in the form of an audio file which can be played back from a computer or tablet. CD is still quite a common format, and you still occasionally see Minidiscs used, but although really popular a few years back, they aren't quite as common anymore. The next section looks at these different types of playback system and notes advantages and disadvantages to each format.

PLAYBACK SYSTEMS

You should already know from your meetings or conversations with the venue or technician, which playback system the venue uses. It important that you supply them with what they need and in the format that they need it.

Compact Disc (CD) - For many years, CD's were the preferred choice for dance shows. Most home computers and laptops had CD writers (burners) built in, and anyone, even with very limited technical ability were able to create, or, 'burn' their own CD's. Many venues or competitions will only give the option of CD playback, but there are a few things you need to know about making a CD, to make sure that they will be able to play the disc you give them.

There are 2 types of domestic recordable compact discs, there is the CD-R, which stands for Compact Disc Recordable and there is the CD-RW, which stands for Compact Disc Re-Writeable. The CD-RW is less common these days.

When you come to burn a CD from your computer, depending on which software you use (Nero and Roxio are both very common programmes to let you create CD's), you will usually be given the option to burn a, 'data disc', or an, 'audio disc'.

Although both data discs and audio discs use the same physical type of blank CD (either CD-R or CD-RW), when you burn a data disc, you are recording the actual computer files to the disc, rather than converting them as audio, to be playable as an audio CD. Only a computer will be able to read this information and you won't be able to play the CD on a standard, domestic CD player, which will only read the CD Audio file.

When you burn your music as an audio disc, the software automatically converts the audio file from your computer to a CD Audio file which is then burnt to the disc, which will then allow you to play back your music on a CD player - provided that the disc is finalised.

For a CD player to be able to read the information on an audio CD, the disc needs to be, 'finalised'. This is where a small bit of data is recorded to the disc, that gives the player some information about the disc's content. If the disc isn't finalised, then although a computer may be able to read the disc, a standard, domestic CD player probably won't even recognise that you have put the disc in. Once a CD-R is finalised, you cannot add any more information (or music) to it. Most CD writing software will automatically finalise the disc for you, some may give you the option to add more music at a later date, or, 'keep the session open'.

A CD-RW will let you add data or audio and then allow you to record over that information until you finalise the disc. Like the CD-R, if the disc isn't finalised, you won't be able to play it on a standard CD player, so there is no advantage to using CD-RW over CD-R.

When recordable CD's first became available in the domestic market, you could record up to 74 minutes of audio on a disc, which is the same as a manufactured music CD that you commercially buy. In recent times, it is more common for blank CD's to be 80 minutes long.

If your show is made up of two parts, a first half and a second half, and if each part is under 74 or 80 minutes (depending on the length of the CD) long each, then it makes sense to make one CD for the first half and one for the second half. Simple so far.

If your first half is more than the length of your CD, then it is probably better if the music for that half is burnt to multiple CD's, with a new CD or CD's being used for the second half.

The reason for this is, if for example, there were 20 songs in your first half, but only 15 would fit onto your disc, the last 5 songs from the first half would be on the second CD. If you were to continue using the same CD for the second half, the first piece of music for the second half would be track 6 on your CD. This isn't really a problem, but if you happen to be rehearsing out of show order and you want to rehearse maybe the fourth number in the second half, in this case, that would be track 9 on your CD. If you suddenly had to swap to a backup disc in the middle of the show, it just makes it easier if the numbers of the show relate to the track numbers of the CD.

It is also very useful to provide a printed list for the sound operator, along with the CD / CD's, with track numbers and titles etc. Some dance schools like to have a play off track for some routines, so for example, if track one on the CD was the first number in the show and track two on the CD is the play off for the first number, then the second routine of the show is actually track three. You can see how this could potentially be a bit confusing the further you get into the show when trying to play the correct tracks in the correct order. Make sure on your printed sheet that it clearly shows exactly what track on the CD relates to which number in the show. Also, if the track is titled one thing but the dance piece is titled another, make sure this is documented too. This might sound obvious, but it is amazing how often this causes problems. The dance teacher may ask for the title of the dance piece, but that doesn't correspond to the title of the track.

An issue I come across over and over again is unlabeled CD's. Many a time, I have been operating sound for dance shows or festivals that feature many different schools, and often get handed a CD that isn't labelled in any way. On some occasions, I could have up to ten or even more CDs for a single show, so always make sure your CD's are clearly labelled with the name of the school / studio and the name of the production or the tracks if needed. You can write on recordable CD's with any waterproof pen, such as a Sharpie.

Another very common problem is that some of the CD's used are of the cheapest quality and often aren't in any sort of protective cover or case. Cheaper ones especially are very easy to scratch. It doesn't take a lot of surface damage for a CD to skip or just not play. Also, the way CD's are burnt on home computers is different to how commercial CD's that you buy are made. Commercially released CD's are, 'pressed' and are of a much higher quality, rather than, 'burnt' CD's, the result being that some players can struggle playing the burnt discs unless they are in good condition.

When burning a CD, if the computer gives you the option of selecting the burning speed (how fast it will take to burn the tracks to the blank CD), always choose the lowest speed available. In an ideal world, burn it at 1 x speed or 2 x speed. This though isn't always an option, but it's something to keep an eye out for. I won't go into technical details of why it is better to burn blank CD's at lower speeds, but the faster it is burnt, the more potential problems a CD player can have in reading and playing the disc. Don't forget to finalise the disc, or at least check that it has automatically finalised.

Always create a backup CD / CD's too, just in case there are any problems. Make sure they are exactly the same as the main CD's and labelled the same, but are also clearly labelled as, 'Back Up'.

Another very common mistake is by trying to use a blank DVD rather than a blank CD. Many a time someone has asked me to burn some songs onto a CD for them, but have actually given me a blank DVD. If it doesn't say on the disc itself, there is a very easy way to check if your blank disc is a CD or DVD by looking at the side that has the information on it, rather than the side with the label. A blank CD is usually silver in colour, where as a blank DVD is slightly more purple in colour. This isn't the case 100% of the time, but it certainly is most of the time.

Minidisc - This was a relatively short-lived format, but you still get the occasional school / studio who prefer to use them. Similar to a CD, the information is stored or burnt on a disc, but it's smaller than a standard CD and also has a square protective plastic casing around it. When minidisc's first appeared on the market, there was a lot of publicity regarding the quality. Simply put, if you had an audio file that you would burn to an audio CD, all of the information burnt onto the disc would be what you ended up with. With minidisc, it was slightly different. It used clever algorithms to analyse the recording to preserve space, a form of digital compression.

It would effectively remove the parts of the audio or data, that it thought weren't needed. For example, if you were in a room and someone was talking quietly on the telephone and suddenly you started playing very loud music so you couldn't hear the person on the phone, if you took a snap shot recording of that room, you would only hear the music, but the person talking would still be there, even if not heard. A minidisc would only record the sound of the loud music, rather than the person on the phone as well, as it assumes it cannot be heard. This seems like a good idea, but the earlier models weren't that great in doing it without noticing that it had affected the audio in some way.

To be honest, as time went on, the quality did get a lot better. There were some advantages to using minidisc over CD, in the fact that they were a lot more robust, you could jump up and down next to the table with the player on and they didn't skip like a CD would. Also, having the plastic protective cover, the discs never got scratched. The biggest advantage was that you could do basic editing on them and name the tracks and they were re - recordable. You could add tracks to them, erase tracks, change the order etc. which was quite appealing at the time.

One problem that did happen on more than one occasion was, similar to a CD, the disc needed to be finalised in order to play it on other players, but unlike CD, once finalised, on a minidisc, you could still go back and add tracks, delete tracks etc. The finalising on the minidisc was done in a slightly different way to CD, in the fact that every time you ejected the disc, it would automatically update the 'TOC' or, 'Table of Contents', which did a similar thing as finalising was to a CD, it was a way of telling the player how many tracks were on the disc, how long they are etc. The problem was if for some reason when ejecting the minidisc, the player didn't write the TOC to the disc, when you next put in the minidisc into the player, it would have no reference to what was on the disc, and therefore, making it unplayable. You still occasionally see gigging musicians, especially club artists who need to play backing tracks use minidisc, as they are small and really robust. If you do still use minidisc, make sure you check with the venue that they have the ability to play them.

Computer Playback - In this day and age, the majority of sound, especially in professional venues is played back from a computer, using some sort of playback software. There are lots of pieces of software that will do this fairly easily and for free, iTunes, Media Player etc. but some are designed especially for this type of application. Probably the most common playback software in theatres around the world (excluding some of Europe for some reason), is a piece of software called, QLab, made by a company called, Figure 53. The only disadvantage with QLab, is that it is for the Apple Mac only, and not available on a PC. The advantage of QLab is that you can download the basic playback program for free. Although many of the clever options are disabled in the free version, you can still use it to run a dance show quite happily.

If the venue is using QLab as their playback format, and if you own an Apple Mac, you could always preprogram the show for the operator, so on the day of rehearsals, you turn up with the QLab file on a USB drive. The operator just needs to transfer the files to their computer and instantly, there is your show.

There is a short tutorial on building your show in QLab later in the book.

For Windows computer users, there is a popular program called SCS (Show Cue System) that is relatively inexpensive. I personally have never used it, but I believe it is fairly user friendly and does everything you would need to do for a dance production and more.

As with any computer media, there are many different formats, and music is no different. You should already know what format you should provide to the sound operator if they are using the computer for playback from the initial meetings.

With audio, the four most common formats that you are likely to come across are, WAV, MP3, MP4 and M4A. Not going into full detail as to how they all work and how they differ from each other, but the WAV file, out of the four mentioned is the higher quality file. When a sound is turned into a WAV file, it doesn't get rid of any of the audio information, and saves it as full quality. Both MP3's and M4A's are compressed files, which means that that the computer does come clever calculations and compresses the file to make it's physical size smaller.

A three minute WAV file is around 30MB in actual size, where as an MP3 / M4A is about 3MB in size. It is compressed by approximately a factor of ten (depending on the quality settings you select when saving). MP4 is also a compressed file, just like the MP3, but it is also often associated with video as well as audio. MP3's are more common on portable music devices due to their much smaller size. You can fit about ten times as many MP3's on a device than you can a WAV file. MP3's also tend to be more widely used in the dance world, as it's much easier and quicker to email an MP3 file to someone - a student, a competition, a venue etc. than it is to email a WAV file, due to the physical size of the file. Depending on the quality settings, it can be very difficult to actually tell the difference between a full quality WAV file and a compressed, good quality MP3, MP4 or M4A file.

The M4A file is an, 'Apple Thing'. It's the format that you often get when downloading from iTunes. There is nothing wrong with using this file format, but be aware that some computers may struggle to play them. Although most computer playback software will play most formats (including many others not mentioned above), always ask the advice of the technician, who should be able to advise you with what works best of their system. Don't assume that all computers can play all file types.

Although not as popular these days, occasionally you still come across, 'WMA' files. I would always try and avoid these if possible. WMA stands for, 'Windows Media Audio' and contains information embedded into the file called, 'DRM' which stands for, 'Digital Rights Management'. It was designed as a copyright tool, trying to stop people copying music and often won't allow you to play the audio file on any computer other than the one it was downloaded on. Often, it won't let you burn a WMA file to a CD.

If you have files from iTunes that are, 'M4P' files, rather than, 'M4A' or, 'MP3', then these may cause issues too. The M4P file also contains the DRM protection and won't let you play on any other machine other than the one you downloaded it on, in fact, they won't even play on the machine you downloaded it on if you're not logged into the same iTunes account that you used to buy it.

You may also come across an AIFF file. This is almost exactly the same as a WAV file, it's just Apple's own version of it. Originally WAV files were exclusively on Windows computers, but that is no longer the case.

HOW TO SUPPLY & LABEL THE MUSIC IF USING COMPUTER

If we have discovered that the venue uses computers to play back the music, and we have been told which format they prefer, depending on which software they happen to use, you need to provide them with the audio files. The easiest way is to put them onto a USB thumb drive or similar. You could also upload them to a Dropbox location too, just check with the venue which they would prefer.

You can save a lot of time if you label the audio files in a sensible way, rather than just leaving them as they were when you downloaded them. For example, if you happened to be doing some routines using the songs from, 'The Greatest Showman', rather than just provide the files as you downloaded them, which will usually just be the name of the song, 'The Greatest Show', 'Never Enough', 'This Is Me' etc. rename them in a way that it is obvious of the running order of them in your show, because if you don't, they will just appear in alphabetical order when transferred to the sound playback computer.

So, for example, using the three songs mentioned, if, 'This Is Me' is the first number in the first half in your show, then, 'Never Enough' is the second, with, 'The Greatest Show' being the third, re name the files (all computers will let you rename files, usually it's done with a right click on the mouse and selecting rename) as, '1.01 This Is Me', '1.02 Never Enough' and, '1.03 The Greatest Show'. The 1 shows which half of the show the track is in, the 01 shows that it's the first track in the show and then the title is the name of the song. If a track was the fifth number in the second half, you would label it as, '2.05' followed by the title. If you do that, they will all be in the correct order when the technician views them. The reason I suggest putting, '01' or, '02' etc. as the track number, rather than, '1' or '2', is that if you have more than ten tracks in that half, any numbers labelled above 10, will show before track number 2 when viewed on a computer. As with using CD, it is still really useful, even when using audio files on a computer to provided printed information about the tracks too, just to be double safe.

FILE FORMAT INFORMATION

It's worth mentioning that all of the above-mentioned file formats, WAV, MP3, M4A etc. also have a number of quality parameters that they are saved in. Some venues and software will only accept or be able to play these files when saved at a particular quality.

It may be that you never have any need to save these files yourself, as you may have just downloaded them and use them how they came, but certainly if you start editing audio tracks, you will need to know what template to save the files as.

There is no right or wrong, but if you stick to the parameters mentioned below, you won't go far wrong.

WAV - 44.1KHz, 16 Bit Stereo

MP3 / MP4 / M4A - 44.1KHz, 192000 bps Stereo

Depending on the software you are using, it might say something like 44 100Hz rather than 44.1KHz - it's the same thing, just as 192000 bps is the same as 192Kbps.

If when saving to MP3 / MP4 / M4A, it doesn't give 192000bps or 192Kbps as an option, always go for the highest number there. These will probably be either, 256000bps (256Kbps) or 320000bps (320Kbps). Either of these are fine, the higher the number, the better the quality, but also the better the quality, the bigger the file size. Also remember to check that it says, 'stereo', rather than, 'mono'.

This may seem quite confusing at the moment, but there is an online video which covers basic editing and saving to different file formats if you want to know more.

EDITING

Even if you're not over confident with computers in general, a little sound editing ability can go a long way when it comes to preparing your music for a production. A few simple edits can be the difference between a fast paced, enjoyable slick show, to a long drawn out, 'when is it going to end' type of show. Just because a song may be 7 minutes long, with a boring middle section, doesn't mean you need the whole 7 minutes.

It may be that you want to cut out a verse, repeat a chorus, fade out at a certain point in the song or maybe you just want one piece of music to fade into another. Whatever you want, it is usually pretty quick and very easy to do.

Often, if competing in dance competitions, there will be a time limit on a piece of music. Even basic editing knowledge can save you the trouble from using an external person to edit your track.

Something as simple as a short fade out will make your piece sound a lot better than just stopping the track at a certain point in the music.

In addition to basic editing, most editing software will also allow you to put on basic effects, such as reverb, delay or echo etc. or even reverse the file so you can play it, or a section of it backwards.

There are a number of sound editing software packages available, many of which cost quite a lot of money. My personal favourites are, Sound Forge and Vegas Video. Although Vegas Video is sold as a video editing package, the audio editing part of it is excellent. They are made by a company called, Magix.

There are also some good free ones out there for both PC and Mac. The most popular free audio editor is, 'Audacity'. The beauty of this software is it's easy to use, it doesn't take long to learn the basic features, and it's free.

MAKING A FADE OUT EDIT IN AUDACITY

Here is a very quick example to show how simple it is to make a track fade out at a certain point in the music. This is also demonstrated in a video on the website in more detail.

Step 1: Go to Audacity's webpage at www.audacityteam.org and follow the links to download the version for your computer - either Windows or Mac.

Step 2: Follow the instructions to install the program onto your computer.

Step 3: When you open the program, the screen will look something like the following image.

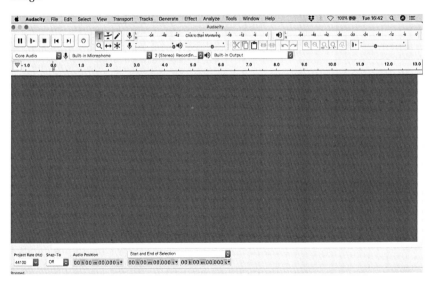

Step 4: Drag your audio file from its folder on your computer onto the large grey area. You will get a pop-up box asking how you want to import the audio file. It will give you three options. For this example, choose option 1, 'Make a copy of the files before editing (safer)'. The reason for doing this, is that if you mess up in anyway and accidentally hit save, you will not have recorded over your original file, as it would have made a copy

of the file for you to work on. Once you have clicked on the, 'ok' box, the screen will look something like this

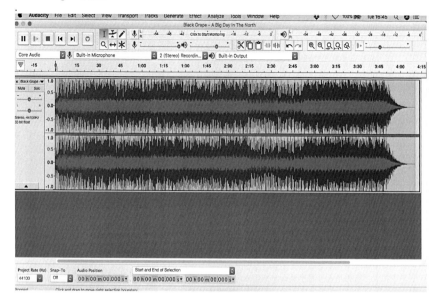

Step 5: Many of you may well be aware of what a sound file looks like, but if not, the spiky, funny looking thing that has just appeared in your Audacity main window is a visual representation of the sound wave file. Although it looks quite complicated, it really is not. The horizontal plane of the file is time - you can see the numbers at the top of the file, this is the time line of the track. The above file you will see is approximately 4 minutes long. If we zoomed in on the file, we could see the exact timings. The vertical plane is level, or loudness. You will notice a number of repetitive spiky peaks, these show that there is a peak in level or loudness at those points. It maybe that these spikes represent a snare drum beat or anything loud and regular. The more you work on editing files, the more you will realise how simple it is and before long, just by looking at the file, you will be able to tell where each section of the song is in relation to the visual image. You will notice in the top left-hand corner of the window are the transport controls to control the audio. These are, Pause, Play, Stop, Back, Forward and Record. To play the file from the beginning just click on the play button. You can also hit the space bar to play and also to stop. You can jump to any part of the file by clicking your cursor anywhere within it and then play again from there.

Step 6: Let's say for example, we want to fade out the track after the music change at around 2 minutes 40 seconds. By using the mouse, left click and highlight the part of the track you want to delete, in this case, it's from around 2 minutes 40 seconds, all the way to the end. When you highlight a section of the track, that section goes white.

Once you highlight an area, that is the area that will be affected by whatever effect or command you tell it to do, in this case, we want to delete it, so just hit the delete key. Once deleted, the file will look like this.

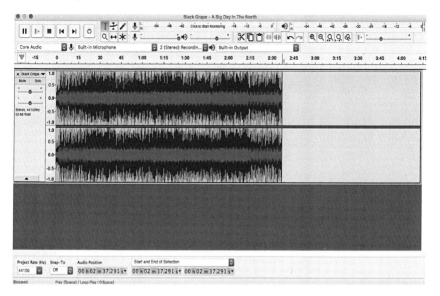

Step 7: If we play that file now, it will just stop at the end point, so we want to put in a short fade just prior to it stopping. In the same way as we selected a section in the last step, we highlight a small section before the end of the track to the end, then at the top of the screen is a drop-down menu called, 'Effect'. Within the drop-down options, you will see one labelled, 'Fade Out'. If you select this, it will put a fade out over you highlighted area.

It might take a bit of trial and error at first to get the exact fade out point and stopping point that you want, but with a little bit of practice, it won't be long before you will be able to identify the different sections in the music just by looking at the waveform file on the screen and making perfect edits without even thinking about it.

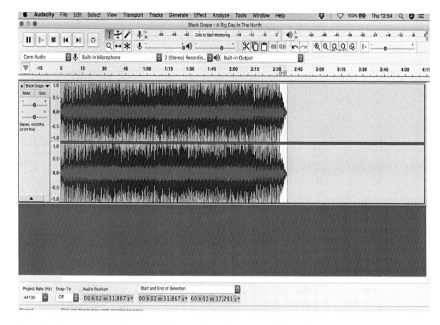

Step 8: Once we are happy with our edited version of the file, we need to save it to a format that our playback system can use. As previously mentioned, WAV and MP3 are the most popular. If you are going to email the edited track to someone, it is probably better saving it as an MP3, as mentioned in a previous chapter, the file will be about a 1/10 of the size of a WAV file.

To save, or convert this new edit to an MP3 or WAV, you need to click on the, 'File' dropdown menu at the top, and then select, 'Export'. This will then give you the option of which file type to save to.

If you are exporting as an MP3, make sure it is selected in the, 'File Type' box, then in the, 'Quality' box, select, 'Extreme 220 - 260 kbps. If you are exporting as a WAV file, make sure you select, 'WAV' in the, 'File Type' box and select, 'WAV (Microsoft) signed 16-bit PCM'.

It's worth noting, that if you have only just installed Audacity, to enable it to save in MP3 format, it needs you to download an external piece of software first called LAME, which is free to download and use, but can't be included with Audacity as they don't own the copyright to the encoder. You will be directed to a download link for this software the first time you try to save a file as an MP3 in Audacity.

Download either the Windows or Mac version of the software and run it. You will then need to close down your saving settings box in Audacity for it to register that you have made a change. If you try to export the file now as an MP3, this time, it will let you do it.

That's it, your file is ready to go. If you search on YouTube for, 'Audacity Tutorial', there are plenty on there that will cover most questions you have about the software.

HOW TO MAKE A QLAB WORKSPACE

If you happen to have a Mac computer, and if QLab is the venue's playback software of choice, or even if you are putting on a show and want to compile and operate the music yourself, here is a quick tutorial on how to very easily and very quickly create a QLab workspace.

In my opinion, QLab is one of the biggest and most influential things that has happened in the theatre sound industry for years. Not only is it an amazing piece of software, it's also incredibly easy to use.

Even better still, the basic version of QLab is free and will do most of what you need to do for your show. It is also very useful for creating playlists for your rehearsals.

Step 1: Go to Figure 53's website - www.figure53.com It will look something like this.

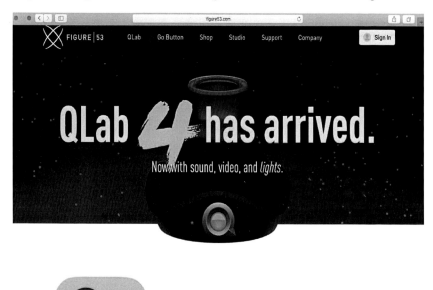

Step 2: Click on the link at the top where it says, 'QLab' and follow the links to download the latest version of the software. It will give you the option to both download and buy. At the time of writing this, version 4 is the current version. Click to download and install it onto your computer.

Step 3: Open up QLab on your computer. The first time you open it, a window will pop up and on the left-hand side of the screen, it will give you three options, these are, 'Open Workspace', 'New Workspace' and, 'Licenses'.

If you are making a new workspace, click on, 'New Workspace'. If you have already made your workspace then click on, 'Open Workspace' to open your show. For this example, we will click on, 'New Workspace'.

You can ignore the licenses option if you're using the free, basic version.

Step 4: Once you have selected, 'New Workspace' in the options, your new, blank workspace will look something like this.

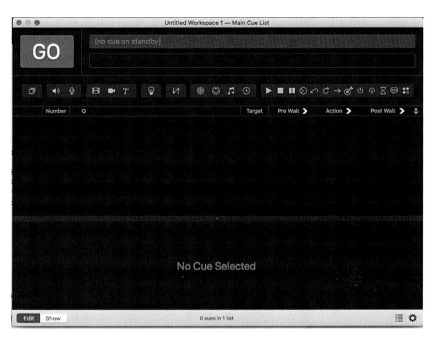

In the bottom, right hand corner, you will see the, 'Settings' icon. This is the circular, cog like icon. Click on this to go to the settings page.

Step 5: On the left-hand side of the window, you will see a number of options. Click on the 2nd option down, which is labelled, 'Audio'. This is where you select your sound output. You will see that in this example, once you have clicked on the, 'Audio' option, next to where it says, 'Audio Patch 1', it says, 'Built in Output'. This is what you need to make sure is selected if you are using your headphone socket on your computer to connect to the mixing desk, or loudspeaker.

If by, 'Audio Patch 1', it says, 'No Device', click on the arrow to the right of the box to give you a drop-down window and select, 'Built in Output'. If you have any other sound cards connected to your computer, like I have in this example, that's where you can select to use those instead of the headphone socket. You don't need to worry about this. Once you have done this, click on the, 'Done' button in the bottom right hand corner of the window. This will close the settings window and take you back to the main blank workspace.

Step 6: Now it's time to start importing your music. This is very simple. Open your finder window on your computer and navigate to where your music is stored and drag and drop the audio file of the first song of the show onto your workspace.

You will now see your song in the workspace. For this example, my first piece of music is, 'Footloose'. You will notice that I have already renamed the track, '1.01 Footloose' as mentioned in the chapter about supplying your music. You don't have to re name your music, especially if it's you who is putting together the QLab workspace, but it's still good practice and keeps your files in a logical order on your computer.

Once you have dragged your track into the workspace, it is now ready to be played. You need to make sure that the track you want to play is highlighted. If it isn't, just click on it, then either click the, 'Go' button on the top, left hand side of the screen, or hit the space bar. This will then play your track. To stop it, hit the, 'Escape' key on your keyboard.

Notice the bottom section of the window, you will see a number of tabs, 'Basics', 'Triggers', 'Time & Loops', 'Audio Levels', 'Audio Trim' and, 'Audio Effects'. These relate to various different settings and parameters of the music track which is highlighted. In this case, 'Footloose'. If there were more tracks in there, it would relate to whichever track you had selected and highlighted.

With this free, basic version, you don't really need to worry about any of these settings, apart from possibly the one labeled, 'Audio Levels'. If you click on the, 'Audio Levels' tab, it will look something like this.

This is where you can control the volume level of your track. You will see there are 3 faders. 'Master', '1' and, '2'. The only fader that you probably may need to play with, is the one labeled, 'Master'. This controls the overall level of your sound file. The, '1 and 2' faders relate to the, 'Left and Right' stereo file.

If your track is too loud, click on the yellow level slider line on the master fader, keep your button clicked on your mouse or pad, and drag the slider down. This will turn down your track. You can use this feature to level out the volume of the songs if your tracks are varying in level.

Continue dragging and dropping all of your songs in order onto the workspace. If you put one in the wrong place, you can change the order within QLab by simply dragging and dropping them.

You can click on any of the songs in your workspace to play, but you will notice that when you play it, the next track down will become highlighted. This means that the next song is cued up ready to go, so next time you hit, 'Go' or the space bar, the highlighted track will play. Be aware that if you play a track and want to change the volume level, the information at the bottom refers to the currently highlighted track. For example, if you play the first track, and want to change the volume level, you will need to click onto that track before you change the level, as it would have automatically cued up for the next track.

Step 6: Now you have got your show in order, don't forget to save the workspace on your computer by clicking on the, 'File' drop down menu at the top left of the screen and selecting the, 'Save As' option.

This will then ask you to give it the workspace a name and ask where you want to save the file on your computer.

Although QLab is a very stable piece of software, it is always worth saving your workspace twice, so you have a backup if anything goes wrong with your file. The backup is usually saved as the same name as the main file, but with the letters, 'BU' after the name.

Step 7: If it's only you who will be operating QLab from your own machine, there is no need to do anything else, but if you want to give the file to a venue, you need to, 'Bundle the Workspace'. When you bundle the show, QLab takes all of the files and information that you have used in your workspace and puts them all together in a folder, which you can then put onto a USB drive and give to the venue. Select, 'Bundle Workspace' from the drop down, 'File' menu as before when you were saving your workspace. It will then ask you where you want to save it.

Depending on how many audio files you have in your workspace, it could take a few minutes to bundle, but once done, it will have created a folder (in the location you told it to bundle to) with the workspace file, and another folder inside containing all of the audio files. This can now be passed on to whoever to use on their own machine. This is also a very good way to archive your show in case you ever want to do it again.

Finally, QLab can do lots more clever things, such as fade outs, controlling other devices, video, lighting and much more, many of the features you need to pay for, but for compiling the music for the show, it is perfect and free. There is a short video on the website going over this exercise in a little more detail.

FOLDBACK

Foldback is the bugbear of many a performer and sound operator. It is the name given to the sound that is played back to the performer through speakers facing them on stage, enabling them to hear it better, rather than the relying on just hearing it from the speakers that are pointing into the audience. Most professional venues will automatically have some sort of foldback system in place, but it might be worth checking when you make your first contact.

It is also worth checking where the venue have their foldback speakers in relation to the stage. If for example, the foldback speakers are just off the stage, down at the front, but during a routine, most of the dance is taking place at the back of the stage and it's a noisy tap routine, it might be difficult for the dancers to still hear the music over the taps, making it hard to stay in time. If the foldback speakers were at the back of the stage and all the action was at the front, you could have the same problem.

A good foldback set up is when the sound is sent back to stage with a fairly even coverage, no matter where the performer is standing or dancing. Bear in mind that the sound operator probably won't be able to tell how loud or quiet the music is from where they are located, as they will be just hearing the sound from the main audience speakers, so if it's too quiet or too loud, make sure you tell them, as they are not mind readers. This might seem obvious, but I have had so many occasions where performers or dance teachers have complained to each other behind the scenes about the level of the music onstage, but never actually said anything to the sound operator.

Foldback When Using Microphones - Unlike a music concert or gig, where the vocalist will want to hear lots of their own vocals onstage to enable them to hear themselves over the rest of the band, in theatre, it is more traditional not to put the vocals of the singer through the foldback system, just the music. The main reason for this is, in a theatre space, where we're not usually playing music as loud as if it were in a club or large venue, any sound fed back to stage will be noticeable to some extent from the audience, or at least to some of the audience.

Why is this a problem? Your brain starts doing funny things to sound when it starts hearing the same sound from different sources and out of time. Sound is relatively slow in the speed it travels. It travels at approximately 343 meters per second or 1125 feet per second under usual atmospheric conditions, although it does change slightly with temperature change, whereas light travels at approximately 299792458 meters per second or 983571056.43 feet per second - quite a difference you may see. What that means is, when sound arrives at your ears from multiple sources at different times, for example if a loudspeaker is 5 meters away from you, and there is also another one at 10 meters away from you being used as a foldback speaker that is still loud enough for you to hear, because there is a 5 metre difference between the two speakers, the sound from the foldback speaker will arrive at your ears 14.5 milliseconds later than the sound from the main speaker (approximately 2.9 milliseconds per metre). That might not sound like a problem, but once that starts happening and sound becomes out of time alignment, it starts effecting the sound with all sorts of crazy phasing effects, which is more noticeable on vocals rather than music. Another reason for not putting much, or any vocals through the foldback is the dreaded, 'Feedback'.

FEEDBACK

This the nasty, usually high-pitched squeal you sometimes hear when a microphone is too loud or the performer walks in front of a loudspeaker. Feedback is created when the sound from the microphone goes through the speaker, which is then picked up by the same microphone, which then goes through the speaker again, which is picked up again by the same microphone and on and on, causing what is known as a, 'feedback loop' or more commonly as just, 'feedback'.

There are three main causes of feedback. These are; 1 - bad loudspeaker placement (for example, the loudspeakers being located behind the vocalist), 2 - the microphone input being turned up too loud on the sound mixing desk and 3 - the vocalist standing too close to a loudspeaker (or pointing a microphone at a loudspeaker).

The only thing that you as a performer can deal with is the, not standing too close to a speaker and not insisting that your vocals are too loud in the foldback speakers. The rest is down to the overall sound system and the sound operator, things that you probably don't have any control over.

Saying all of that, it is not to say that you can't have the vocals through the foldback. Often it is a necessity to be able to pitch correctly, but be aware that if a vocalist walks in front of a loudspeaker with their microphone turned on and it does cause some feedback, there is not a lot the operator can do, apart from turn the mic off.

MICROPHONES

Microphones come in all different shapes and sizes, and different types are used for different things. There are many that you may come across when putting on a dance show, but I'll talk about the most common. Many people still don't understand what microphones can and cannot do for a production, they think that they are the magic solution for getting everything and everyone heard. This is often not the case.

Float Microphones - Float mics is the term given to microphones placed at the front of the stage, that are mostly used for picking up taps or bringing out voices a little when singing towards the front of the stage. These can be really quite effective when used correctly, but don't work very well when you get further away from them. The most common type of float mic is the Crown PCC 160, which is a 'plate microphone' or more correctly, a, 'PZM' (Pressure Zone Microphone) or, 'Boundary Microphone'. It sits on the floor and uses a flat plate to reflect the sound into the microphone capsule. It is quite traditional in a dance show to maybe have 3 of these mics towards the front of the stage - one on centre and the other two either side of the centre one, about 1/3 of the stage apart.

All microphones have what is called a, 'Polar Response Pattern'. This refers to how and where the microphone picks up the sound around it. There are 4 basic polar response pattern shapes, these are;

Omnidirectional – this is where the microphone picks up the sound evenly all around. It can pick up the sound from the front, the back, the side fairly evenly.

Bi-Directional (also known as figure of eight) – this is where the microphone can pick up the sound evenly from the front or the back of the microphone, but not so much from the sides.

Cardioid – this is a heart like shape response, where the sound is picked up well from the front, not too bad from the sides, but not very well from behind.

Hyper Cardioid – this is very similar to the cardioid response, but is a bit tighter and stretched, so really focusses on the sound that is directly in front of the mic, but not so much from the sides and not a lot from behind.

These boundary microphones have an omnidirectional response, so can pick up evenly all around it. The thing to remember about all microphones is, they can't tell the

difference between what they are meant to pick up and make louder, and what they are not meant to pick up. If for example, you had some float mics at the front of the stage to use to pick up small children singing, they would not only pick up the voices, but also any shuffling of feet on the floor and also the music that they are singing along to. Saying that, as long as they are used correctly, they can be really useful for your routine, especially for a tap number.

Crown PCC 160

One thing to be aware of, is dancers stamping on them. The mics are usually placed a little further to the front of the stage than the dancers actually go, so make sure if using them, you let your dancers know what they are and where they are. If they do happen to hit one with their feet and it's turned on, it will make a very loud bang and quite possibly damage the microphone. Also remember that these microphones don't work miracles, they are only there to support. If you are using them to amplify some voices near the front of the stage, it doesn't mean that the singers don't have to sing out loud as if the mics weren't there. If they are singing quietly, the sound operator ends up trying to turn the microphones up. They then pick up the music, which then goes through the speakers, which then gets picked up again by the mic, then goes through the speakers again and so on, and just like I mentioned before, the dreaded feedback will occur again. If you want to get a big vocal sound over the music, this type of float mic at the front of the stage are not usually the correct tools for the job.

Another popular type of float microphone is the, 'shotgun mic'. These are long, thin

microphones and they usually have a cardioid or hyper cardioid response, so they are good at picking up directly what is in front of them. These microphones are usually positioned along the front of the stage on small stands, rather than actually sat on the floor like the boundary microphones. They are probably a better option if you are using floats to pick up voices on stage, and are often used for choirs. If

Shotgun Microphone

you are using the floats mainly for taps, the boundary mics are usually the better option.

Dynamic Microphone - This is what you would expect to see when talking about a standard stage microphone. It's usually hand held and has a cable plugged in to the end, which then goes off to the sound desk. There are many different types of dynamic microphones, but the one you will probably see most often is the, 'Shure SM58'. This is a great work horse of a microphone, it's robust, it's relatively cheap, it sounds pretty good and can withstand high pressure levels going into it, so it won't get damaged if

Shure SM58

you suddenly scream down it or put it right next to a kick drum. The disadvantage of this of course, is that it has a trailing lead coming out of the end of it, probably going all of the way off stage somewhere. If the microphone was to sit in a stand for the duration of the show or there wasn't a lot of movement with it, it might be absolutely fine, but if it's being used for a song and dance, where the vocalist is moving all over the stage, it's probably not the right microphone for this occasion.

RADIO MICROPHONES

This is where it starts to get a little bit complicated and potentially very expensive. Radio mics, or wireless mics as they are also often referred to, can be brilliant for many applications. Not a large-scale theatre show goes by these days without tens of radio mics being used, but if not used correctly, they can sound worse than if not used at all, and can potentially cause no end of problems. There are also strict laws about using them, and although this should be the sound operator's problem, rather than yours, it's still useful to know a little about them, so you can understand and avoid potential problems.

A radio microphone consists of three parts, the microphone itself, the transmitter pack and the receiver (although a hand-held radio microphone has the transmitter built into the microphone itself, so only two parts), The microphone puts the sound signal into the transmitter, and the transmitter sends the signal over radio waves to the receiver, so no need for cable from the microphone to the sound desk. The receiver is the unit that is tuned to the same frequency as the transmitter and receives the radio waves, turns them back into an audio signal, and is then plugged into the sound desk. Each individual radio microphone transmits on it's own exclusive radio frequency (most professional models allow you to choose a number of different frequencies). Just like you tune a radio to receive a particular radio station, this works in a similar way.

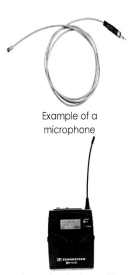

Example of a
microphone

Example of a transmitter

Example of a receiver

To use most radio mics, you need to have a licence to transmit / broadcast on particular frequencies. You shouldn't need to worry about this though, as the venue, or hire company should have the licence. There are some frequencies that you don't need a licence for, but due to the way that the radio microphones work with each other, this will only allow you to use maybe a couple at a time without causing interference, these are rarely used in professional theatre. Different countries have different rules regarding radio broadcasting, but in the UK and Europe, it is overseen by a company called Ofcom.

The standard radio microphone licence that you get in the UK covers a set number of frequencies that you are allowed to use. You are not allowed to use any frequencies that you don't have a license for. Frequencies are split up into bands, known as TV Channels. This isn't like a TV channel, such as BBC 1 or ITV, but a number given to reference a select block of frequencies. The standard radio microphone licence in the UK covers TV Channel 38, which in frequency terms is 606.00 MHz (megahertz) to 614.00 MHz. The standard Chanel 38 licence covers the frequencies within that band, although you can only use between 606.500 MHz to 613.500 MHz as you have to keep at least 500 Hz (hertz) free on each end of the channel.

You cannot use more than one radio microphone on the same frequency, each one has to be exclusive. This is where it starts to get a bit more complicated.

When you transmit on a particular frequency, you are also transmitting to a smaller extent on various frequencies either side of your selected frequency. When only using one radio microphone and receiver, this isn't a problem, but it does become a problem when wanting to use more than one. Frequencies can interfere with each other and cause major problems, such as audio drop outs and strange whistling noises, which is caused by a thing called, 'intermodulation'. Because of this, different manufacturers of radio microphones come with preset frequencies that are designed to be used together without causing these interference problems.

Depending on what make and model of radio microphone you are using, at most, within the standard channel 38 licence, you can use up to a maximum of about 11 microphones. This isn't an exact number as they can still interfere with each other depending on the position of one microphone in relation to another. If you want to use more than around 11 radio microphones, the venue may have to apply for an additional licence for the extra frequencies required.

Unless the venue already owns a licence for the additional frequencies, if you want to use more radio microphones that fit within the channel 38 licence, there is a good chance that the cost will be charged to you.

Once we know how many radio mics we need to use, and made sure we are all legal with correct licences, you need to decide what type of microphone you want and what you want it to do. Like with all microphones, they are not these magic things that make quiet, mumbling singers better, they just allow you to make them louder. Different types of microphones are used for different applications.

The three types of radio microphone you are most likely to come across are;

1 - **Lavalier Microphone** - This is a microphone with a small capsule and a cable (that plugs into the transmitter.) The advantage of a lavalier microphone is, it can be clipped

Example of a lavalier mic

to your lapel, or hidden discretely in your hair line, and the transmitter can be clipped onto your belt or the inside of your costume (or many other places, such as within wigs, strapped to legs, anywhere you can think of where they are out of the way). This is the most popular style of radio microphone in musical theatre. It is also often referred to as a, 'body mic' or, 'head mic'. Often, the cable will be coloured to blend in better with the hair to disguise it a bit more. When being worn in the hair line, there are a number of ways the microphone can be attached, including the use of wig clips or elastic. You will also often see them worn over the ear, usually attached to some sort of plastic hear hanger.

2 - **Headset Microphone** - Similar to the lavalier, but attached to a thin wire frame which clips over the ears and has a short, usually stiff boom to situate the microphone capsule closer to your mouth. The closer the microphone is to your mouth, the bigger and fuller the sound will be, so this style of microphones are more common in louder, rock n' roll jukebox styled musicals. There are different types of headsets you can get,

some discrete designs for use in theatre like the one in the photo, but also some bigger, more noticeable designs, like the, 'Madonna' microphone which are designed for pop music, where it doesn't matter if they are seen and the sound wants to be big and full, while still allowing the performer to dance or move around.

Example of a headset mic

3 - **Hand Held Radio Mic** - This will probably be the most recognisable radio microphone to you, it looks just like a normal stage vocal mic, but is wireless. It is a

microphone and transmitter in one. If it's big sound you want, fighting over loud music, this is the best option. Simply speaking, the bigger the microphone capsule (head) and the closer it is to your mouth will provide the biggest, fullest sound. Take the advice from the sound technician to see what types of radio microphones are available and which would be better for your needs. Remember, the further away from your mouth the microphone is, the more the sound operator will have to

Example of a hand held mic

turn it up, the more chance you will get of feedback, especially if the microphone is also picking up music from your foldback.

THINGS TO BE AWARE OF WHEN USING RADIO MICS

If you are using lavalier or headset radio microphones in your production, be aware that they are very delicate and easy to damage, so always make sure your performers are aware of what they are and even more so, how much they cost. Mis use of a radio microphone can be incredibly expensive for you.

Sweat can cause the microphone not to function correctly. The sweat gets into the capsule of the mic and dulls the sound. This is usually only a temporary problem as once dried out, they are usually fine again. During musical theatre shows, if a mic gets, 'sweated out' as it's often referred as, it is common for the Sound Number 2 (see later chapter) to spray the head of the mic with compressed air, which more often than not will quickly dry the sweat and make the microphone work correctly again.

The transmitter packs can also be affected by heat and sweat. If a transmitter pack is buried deep inside a costume with many layers, they can occasionally overheat and cause the audio to drop in and out. It's worth a performer keeping an eye out on the temperature of the pack. If it starts getting more than a little warm, the positioning of it may need changing. For particularly sweaty performers, it is common for the transmitter to be put inside a non-lubricated condom, or surgical probe cover. This keeps the sweat away from the pack.

Lavalier - If wearing a lavalier microphone on your head, there is no exact position for it, but the sound will be a lot more natural sounding if it is situated below the hairline in the centre, or at least within the window of the outsides of your eyebrows. This may sound strange, but the sound operator will have to do more at his end to make it sound natural if you place it further round your head, and even more so if it is being worn over the ear. It might be that the microphone has to go over the ear, especially if the performer is bald, but just be aware that the sound operator may need a little more time to make it sound more natural.

Headset - This is often the preferred option for dance style shows over the lavalier mic, as it is quite quick and easy to take on and off a performer's head and put on another person. If you don't have enough radio microphones for your needs and are looking at swapping some between performers, this may be a better option.

In a professional production, if a performer is wearing one of these microphones, they will almost certainly also have the frame of the headset pinned into their hair, or at least secured in some way. Be aware that there can be quite a bit of movement of them if not secured. Most headsets are adjustable to a point, but there may be problems if you are sharing a particular microphone between an adult and a small child. The boom arm where the actual microphone part of the headset is, is usually made of very thin metal, this is very easy to bend into place if the microphone in not quite in the correct position - do not do it! It doesn't take much to actually snap the boom arm in the headset and it is also the most expensive part of it to be replace, so treat it with respect and care. Depending on the type of headset a venue may have in stock, especially if it's a professional venue who produce shows, there is a chance that the headset microphone alone could be worth anything between £100 and £500. Bare this in mind when working out who is going to be using which microphone - more on this later.

Hand Held - These are probably the preferred option by the sound operator, but may not be the best option for your routine. They are certainly the easiest to manage by the operator, although they still have to be used correctly, as bad microphone technique can ruin even the best performance.

If for example the routine consists of three children sharing and singing into a single hand held microphone and the child in the centre has it next to their mouth and the other two aren't as close to it as the centre child, only the middle child will be heard. Just the same as if the same three children are singing down the same single mic and the centre child is holding it down by their stomach, none of them are going to be heard. This may sound really obvious, but it's something I come across time and time again. Many times, it doesn't actually matter to the dance teacher, but there is no reason why a little bit of thought or forward planning can't make something that little bit better. It would also be really useful when rehearsing your show, for the singers to get used to passing round microphones, if that's what's going to happen in the actual show. Even if you use something like a piece of thick wooden rod, deodorant can, or even a hair brush, anything like that would get them used to performing with something in their hand and you can work on their discipline to hold it in the right place before you even get into the venue.

When any microphone is set into a sound mixing desk, it's not just a case of plugging it in and away we go. There are a large number of settings that the operator has to do to make it work how it should for that particular application. The first thing they do is to adjust the level coming in from the microphone to an optimised level in the mixing desk to be able to use it correctly. For example, this can mean that if a particular microphone has been set up for a strong voiced male singer, who holds the microphone to his mouth, it will not have the same qualities if that mic is then used by a small, softly spoken child who holds the mic by their chest. Of course, the sound operator is able to turn the level up or down, but there are many settings that can't be done, 'on the fly'.

MAKE A MICROPHONE PLAN

If you are using microphones in your show, be it radio microphones or cabled, it is incredibly useful for the sound operator if you can provide them with a mic plan. This is usually in the form of a simple chart that shows which microphones are used in which routines.

Firstly, if using more than one microphone, the sound operator will almost certainly need to label them in some way, usually by giving each microphone a number. If they are being neat and tidy, they may use a label printer to print out a label with a number on, which is stuck onto the body of the transmitter, or they may just stick a bit of masking tape on the transmitter, with a number written on it. If they are using hand held radio microphones, they may be labelled by a colour, rather than a number.

Many models of hand held microphones can have a coloured ring attached to the body of the mic to help identify it. A hand held microphone could also be identified by a coloured pop shield.

A pop shield is the foam cover that fits over the top of the mic to reduce the extra wind noise when singing or talking down the mic.

The microphone plan is just a simple chart showing which microphones are used in which routine. The simplest way of doing it is to have a table with all of the microphones used labelled along the top, then the name of each routine listed on the side. See the example of how to lay out your plan. You can also download this plan template from the website, where you can edit it to suit your needs.

Studio 97 - Dance 'Till You Drop - Microphone Plan Template

Song	Mic 1	Mic 2	Mic 3	Mic 4	Mic 5	Mic 6	Float Mics
ACT 1							
Greatest Showman	LEAD			BACKING		BACKING	
Over The Rainbow		LEAD					
Disco Inferno							
Bye Bye Blackbird	LEAD						
Black Magic		LEAD 1	LEAD 2	LEAD 3	LEAD 4		
42nd Street							YES
ACT 2							
Les Mis Medley	LEAD 1	LEAD 2	BACKING	BACKING	BACKING	BACKING	
Cats Medley							
Luck Be A Lady			LEAD				YES
My Girl Lollipop							YES
I Know Him So Well		LEAD 1			LEAD 2		
Finale			BACKING		BACKING	BACKING	

You will note that in the column I have written either, 'Lead' or 'Backing', this just refers to lead vocals or backing vocals. It could be that rather than write that, you actually have the performers name instead, or as well as. Just remember that the operator may not know the name of the performers, so don't just rely on that.

In addition to this, if there is a routine where there are a number of vocalists all doing a different line in the song, providing a copy of the lyrics with it clearly marked which vocalist does which line, and what number microphone is used could be a huge help to the operator, especially if they don't know the song or the performer.

WHAT IS A SOUND NUMBER 2?

We mentioned earlier about the different types of radio microphones and also about microphone plans, but a very important role in your show (if using radio microphones) is what is traditionally called in the musical theatre world, the, 'Sound Number 2', or, 'A2' as it is referred to in some other countries, including America.

In a professional theatre musical, there are a number of people who are responsible for the sound of a show. Depending on the scale and budget, these include a, Sound Designer, Associate Sound Designer, Assistant Sound Designer, Production Sound Engineer, Sound Number 1 (also known as Front of House Engineer, or A1) and a Sound Number 2 (also known as Stage Sound, Deck Sound or A2). In some occasions on very large shows, you can even have a Sound Number 3 (A3) and Sound Number 4 (A4).

Although not usually involved in the actual sound of the show itself, the Sound Number 2's job is incredibly important. It is their responsibility to make sure that all radio microphones have fresh batteries for each show, to make sure each mic is correctly distributed to the right performer, to be responsible for monitoring all radio mics throughout the show and to deal with any on stage sound issues. It's also their job to deal with the maintenance and cleaning of the microphones, as they are very delicate, expensive pieces of equipment, and to make sure that all of the radio microphones are fitted to the performer correctly. This is where it becomes important to your show.

If you are intending on using radio microphones in your show, it is important that you have someone performing the role of the Sound Number 2. This could be a member of the venue staff, but it is more advisable to get someone associated with your company to do it. Not only because the children will be more comfortable with someone they know, but it will also mean that you're not paying another wage.

The role of this person in the type of show that you are likely to be putting on, will be to make sure that the correct performer has the correct microphone on at the correct time. Depending on the style of your routine, it could be that it is a classic musical theatre styled piece, where the microphones are fitted in the hair line, either by clips or by a thin piece of elastic around the head, with the microphone knotted into it. It could be that it's a production number style song and the performer is wearing an over the ear, head mic style radio microphone or maybe it's a pop song where the performer is using a hand held microphone. Whichever it is, you need to make sure that the venue technician has gone through with whoever is doing that job for you.

Most microphone transmitter packs have clips that enable them to be clipped onto a belt or trousers etc. It may be that you don't want the microphone transmitter each to be seen, therefore, it may need to be fitted inside the costume, or even clipped to the back of a bra strap.

Ask the venue if they have any radio microphone pouches. These are just material pouches that the transmitter fits inside of, with a chord or strap that can either clip or fasten around the waist of the performer. This is the easiest option, as it's fairly quick to easily swap the transmitter packs between performers if they are sharing microphones.

By far the quickest and easiest option of radio microphones if swapping between performers is the hand held microphone. This can be passed from one person to another. The headset microphone is probably the next quickest option. It just easily sits on the head, over the ears and can be removed very quickly.

The slowest option is by using the lavalier microphones hidden in the hair line. If you are really keen that this is how your microphones are worn by the performer, it is worth asking the venue technician if they have any spare lavalier microphones so the performers can pre fit them into their hair, and then if they need to share transmitters, it's easier just to disconnect the lavalier microphone from the transmitter and swap that, rather than swapping out both transmitter and mic and having to re fit it on the next performer.

It is important that the Sound Number 2 is working to the same mic plan as the person operating the sound for the show. It is also important that they are able to communicate with them via the cans (see terminology section) in case there are any problems with the microphones and you need to change the order of who is wearing which mic. Also, if the wrong mic has been put on someone by mistake, they will need to let the sound operator know quickly, so that they can make the correct microphone live.

Just a couple of final points before we move to the next section. Make sure that you, or at least the person who has been given your Sound Number 2 role, are aware of not only how delicate radio microphones are, but also how expensive they are. Make sure this is drummed into the performers mind. There is nothing worse for a venue to have the performers mis treating and damaging the radio microphone. This is never done intentionally, but it is still easily done, especially with the headset mics. Often, these will have a thin boom arm coming from the ear piece to the mouth, with the actual microphone capsule on the end, which sits near the mouth. It is common for performers who don't realise how delicate and expensive they are to try and bend the boom to make it fit to their face better. Doing so can easily snap them.

Also, due to swapping microphones between performers and maybe slightly ill-fitting headsets, it may be that the microphone capsule is sitting a bit too close to the performer's mouth. If you, or they can hear heavy breathing, wind noise and snorting while the performer is singing, that is a sign that it is too close to their mouth, or nose. There is absolutely nothing that the sound operator can do about this from the sound desk, apart from turn it off. Instruct the performer beforehand that if they hear this during their song, carefully try to reposition the mic slightly further away from their mouth or nose and that should fix the problem.

If the performers are using hand held microphones. Make sure they are all aware of the correct way to hold them. The microphones need to be fairly close to their mouth, but not so much that they are eating the end of it, and don't hold it down by their chest. This may sound obvious, but it's amazing how often singers don't realise that they actually have to sing into the microphone. The most common bad practice with holding hand microphones is the, 'wind screen wiper technique'. This is where the performer thinks they are controlling the level of their voice into the microphone by moving the microphone from side to side or constantly changing the distance between their mouth and the microphone, this isn't really useful unless they happen to be an experienced vocalist performer and know what they are doing.

A common fault with radio microphones, more so with headsets and lavaliers that plug into a transmitter, is sometimes, depending on the type of connector, it can work itself loose, or if not tightened up correctly to begin with, it can cause huge crackle like noises if the microphone is live and turned up on the mixing desk. If this is the case, the operator will usually contact the Number 2 Sound to ask them to check the connector is tightened up correctly.

PRE RECORDING THE BACKING VOCALS

Recorded Vocals - If in your show, there are only a few principal singers who need microphones, but you have some numbers that require multiple backing vocals or a large chorus, one way you may be able to save some money on the radio mic hire costs, is getting somebody to record the additional vocals using your performers. There are many audio services and studios who are able to provide this service, it might also be that the venue can provide the facility too. It may well be cheaper to book a sound engineer for a few hours to record and mix your tracks than it is to hire a large additional amount of radios microphones that only get used in a few numbers. Some people may see this as cheating, but it can still be your students who make the recordings, and technology is there to help us. Many top shows in the West End and Broadway have some additional vocals or instruments prerecorded. It doesn't mean your chorus or backing vocalists won't be singing on the stage, it just means that they will have some additional support. From experience I can say that this can make a routine sound so much better, especially if it's for something like a finale where you have your whole cast singing, but can only afford radio microphones for the principal vocalists.

VIDEO

If you thought that radio microphones were complicated, wait to you start wanting to put video in your show.

My first question would be when planning my show, do I really need video in it, or am I just doing it for the sake of it, and the fact that the last dance school at that venue did it, so we're going to do it too? The reason you should ask yourself this, is that sometimes, unless you have a large budget and plenty of programming time, the end results can be quite disappointing. Saying that, with the right equipment, knowledge and creative input, video can be an excellent inclusion to your production.

There are two types of, 'video' that you will come across. The first is by using projection. This is a signal fed into a projector, projected onto a screen or flat surface. The other is a video wall, which is made up, usually from lots of LED's (small lights) and are incredibly expensive to both buy and even hire. Unless the venue or event that you are performing in has a video wall, the chances are, your only option will be projection. When initially talking about projection with the venue or the technician, there are a number of questions that you need to know the answer to. Apart from the obvious question of if they have a projector and how they want you to submit the images or video, which we will go into later on, and more importantly, how much they will charge you for the hire of it for the duration of your residency. There are questions such as; what size is the projector in terms of light output, resolution and ratio. What are the screen options, do the venue have separate projection screens or will you be wanting to project the images or videos into the cyc at the back of the stage (this is probably the most common). Another very important question is where the projector is physically situated within the space. Is it high above, pointing to the stage on a steep angle, or is it at a lower level at the rear of the auditorium. This is quite an important question, as the answer will determine how shadows from the performers will affect the image. If the projector is too low, no matter where on the stage the performers are, they will almost certainly always be creating shadows on the screen. If the projector is rigged high and pointing down towards the stage, you may be able to almost stand up against the screen without causing a shadow. If using a special, 'BP Screen', or, 'Back Projection Screen', you can project from behind, which would then cause no shadows at all from the projector onto the screen, but in most cases, there just isn't the room on the stage for that to be an option.

There are a number of different ways that your video or images can be fed into the projector. The most basic way is from a pre-made DVD plugged directly into the projector. This is probably the most awkward way of doing it, as someone will have to control the DVD player separately to everything else, very often when you press any command on the DVD player, such as, 'play' or, 'pause' etc. it will show the text on the screen.

A common way, especially if you are only using still shots, rather than video, is through a, 'PowerPoint' or, 'Keynote' presentation, fed from a computer fed directly to the projector. Although there is no problem with doing that, it's very limiting with what you can actually achieve.

By far the most common way at the moment (although technology changes so quickly, it could be completely different in a few years' time - in which case an other edition of this book will be needed), is by using a piece of software such as, QLab.

I mentioned QLab earlier in the sound section. QLab has revolutionised the workings of sound and video in theatres all over the world. I also mentioned that it's Apple Mac based only, so if the venue only uses Windows PC's, then other software will be needed, but the venue or technician should be able to deal with that and advise you accordingly.

The great thing about QLab, as mentioned earlier, is, the basic version is free. Anybody can download the latest version from the, 'Figure 53' web site.

The latest version of QLab (V4 at the time of print), is split into three main areas of control, audio, video and lighting. The free version has the basic features of all three. These are often enough to put on a basic technical show, but it starts getting really clever when you buy the licences to unlock the different features. You can buy a license for any one, two or all three of the main controllers (audio, video & lighting) and also in any combination. For example, you could have the licence for the audio and video features, but just the basic lighting features etc. Another great feature is, you can rent a licence for a set period in 24-hour blocks. For example, if you plot your show in QLab, (see previous tutorial) and you only have the basic, free version, but you need the full features for your production, you don't need to buy the full licence, you can just rent it for a set period of time - your show week for example. The rates are really reasonable too, they work out at a few dollars per feature per day.

The beauty of using QLab for video is that it can do video mapping. This means that you can create different projection surfaces, or areas within the full projected area. For example, if the projector is capable of projecting an image on to the cyc, covering the whole area, within QLab, you can create different areas anywhere within that coverage. This is a little hard to explain without seeing it, so I have included some clips from a show I did a while ago on the web site. In this show, we had four, two metre by two metre projection screens on wheels, that were set in different positions on the stage at different times. As long as the projection screens stayed within the area that the projector could cover, and as long as they were set in the same place each time, we could, 'map' the video to the individual four screens, and project onto one or more of them independently. This means that depending on the spec of the computer (as video takes up a lot of processing power), you can be incredibly creative and have different images or videos on a number of different screens at any one time.

FORMAT, RESOLUTION AND RATIO

Video / Image Format - As with sound, video has lots of different formats, much more than audio. To complicate things even more, each format has lots of different parameters. Luckily, QLab, and most other software can deal with various different formats.

With audio, when you were dealing with WAV, MP3, M4A / M4V, video deals with files such as MPEG 4, AVI, MOV, Pro Res and many more.

In a similar way to an MP3 being a smaller, compressed version of an audio file, such as a WAV file (see earlier section about audio formats), MPEG 4 is also a compressed file, where as a ProRes is an uncompressed file. The advantage of the MPEG 4, is the physical file size is a lot smaller and is probably a more common format, especially for online videos, but due to the compression, the computer has to work harder to play the file (to uncompress it) and sometimes, depending on how powerful the computer is, and on factors such as, playing multiple video files at once etc., the video may not end up playing back smoothly. For QLab, the preferred format is ProRes 422 Proxy.

With pictures or photos, there are also a number of standards, including, BMP, JPEG, PNG, GIF etc. Like audio and video, some of the files are compressed and some aren't, but due to the nature of the relatively small file size, it takes very little processing power to uncompress a compressed picture file, so pretty much any format, providing the software is capable of playing that format is ok to use.

Screen Ratio - This is something to think about when making your videos, or when getting someone to make your videos for you. The screen ratio refers to the size of the width of the video, in relation to the size of the height. Although there are a number of common screen ratios, the two most common you will come across are 4:3 - Standard Ratio and 16:9 - Widescreen. Standard ratio is what most TV sets used to be, not quite square, but almost. Widescreen is what most TV sets are now. The numbers don't relate to an actually size, but to a ratio. For example, an old standard ratio TV set could have a screen that was 40 cm wide and 30 cm high, or 80 cm wide and 60 cm high, both are a 4:3 ratio. Just as a widescreen TV could have a screen that was 160 cm wide and 90 cm high, or 320 cm wide and 180 cm high etc. The majority of projectors project a standard ratio image by default. Many can project in widescreen too. It's important to know which ratio the projector that you're using when creating your video files uses. If you create a widescreen video file and project it using a projector that can only project a standard image then the result will be one of three things. Either, the image will be squashed in a little from the left and right, or, it will be stretched a little up and down, or finally, it could show correctly, but won't fill the whole screen, there will be a gap at the top and the bottom. You may remember when TV sets used to be mostly standard ratio, if ever a widescreen film was shown, there would be black bars at the top and bottom of the screen. One option might be to zoom the image and make it fill the whole screen, but that will result in bits of the sides of the video being cut out. The software you are using can often deal with this, but not always, so it's always best to check.

Resolution - The resolution of an image or video, relates to how many individual pixels the video or photo image is made up from. The higher the resolution, the better quality the image, especially when projected onto a large screen.

A good example to see what is meant my resolution is to go to YouTube and select a video to play. In the bottom right of the playing screen, there is a little cog wheel that is labeled, 'settings' when you hover your cursor over it. This will then give you an option labelled, 'Quality'. When you click on that, you will then get a list of quality options, these refer to the resolution of the video clip. They will be something like, '144p, 240p, 360p, 480p, 720p and 1080p'. Sometimes, they may even have the option of choosing, '4K'.

The number quoted is the number of individual pixels or blocks high the video is split up into. The less the number of pixels or blocks a video is made up of, the lesser the quality it is. This is even more noticeable the bigger you make the image. If you fill the whole screen with a video that only has a resolution of 144, it will look terrible. If you fill it with a video that is at least 720, or better still 1080 (regarded as HD - High Definition), then the quality will be much better.

With pictures or photos, I would be very wary when using an image less than 1000 pixels wide. Some people steal pictures off the internet (more about that in the next section), which are really low resolution, which mean they just look terrible when projected onto a large screen.

Once we have established what format, ratio and resolution our videos or images are to be, we need to start thinking about the content.

STOCK VIDEO / PHOTOS

Just as you have to pay for the use of music in your production to the PRS (Performing Rights Society - explained in a later chapter), you also have to pay for the use of any videos or images that you don't own the copyright to, or at least get the permission of the copyright holder. That means you can't (or at least, shouldn't), just go online, get a load of pictures from the internet and use them in your show. Someone else owns the copyright and they should be paid. Imagine if you had taken a photograph, made a film, or written a song and somebody used it without getting your permission, or more importantly, without paying you to use it, you would probably feel pretty annoyed. The easiest way around this is to buy video or images from a 'Stock' site. A piece of stock video / music / photograph etc., is one where you pay for the licence to use that content in your product. It doesn't mean you then own the copyright of the piece, it just means that the person who created it, will be paid for producing it. There are many stock sites online, such as, Pond 5, Shutterstock, iStock photo and many more. Just do an internet search, and you will find plenty of them. Videos are often more expensive than photos, but neither are usually very expensive, and in buying it, it gives you the peace of mind that you have permission to use it. Just imagine if you were using a video clip from a film or an image that you didn't own and somebody took a video clip of your show and posted it online. If it was ever found out that you didn't have permission to use it, you could potentially end up with a fine of thousands of pounds.

Alternatively, there are also many people who create videos and images who are more than happy for people to use for nothing. YouTube is a great source of, 'royalty free' material, especially video. Just always make sure that you check the descriptions to confirm if there is a price to pay or if there are conditions of use. Some people will allow you to use their work if they get an acknowledgment in the programme or some sort of credit etc.

PYROTECHNICS & OTHER VISUAL EFFECTS

As well as lighting and video projection, there are many ways to create visual effects for your productions.

Pyrotechnics go through phases of popularity. They can be used to quite dramatic effect, but in a similar way to video, have a think if you really need them and if it actually adds to your routine or show, as it's very easy to have them for the sake of it.

There are a number of pyrotechnics (often referred to as pyros) that are used on stage, but the most popular (at a reasonably affordable price) are gerbs, flash pots and smoke pots.

A 'Gerb', pronounced jerb, gives out a burst of vertical sparks. You can buy them by time duration and by colour, so for example, you could have a 3 second, golden gerb, or you could have a 7 second red gerb, or any combination of available timings and colours.

A 'Flash Pot' is a small pot, that when detonated, creates a sort of quick flash effect, the sort of thing you may see in a pantomime when the good fairy or the baddie comes onto the stage. You can get these in a number of different colours too.

A 'Smoke Pot' is similar to the flash pot, but rather than a lit-up flash, it is purely just an instant smoke burst, again, often seen in pantomimes.

There are many other types of stage pyrotechnics available, but the bigger they get, the more expensive they get. Another smaller pyrotechnic, is a 'Robot'. Although not as common in dance shows, these give an instant short burst of sparks, similar to how we expect an electrical fault to look like, like a fuse box blowing up.

Fire is quite a fun way to liven up a show and there are a number of affordable fire products available. In a similar way that a gerb gives a vertical burst of coloured sparks over a duration of time, you can get 'Flame Projectors', which are a similar thing, but this time with fire. Similar to the gerb, once the flame projector has been detonated, it gives a vertical flame of a particular colour for the set duration.

If you want to get more creative with fire, you can buy or hire various different flame effect devices. One example is the, 'Salamander' by a company called, Le Maitre. This is a metallic, rectangular box, with a type of gas canister inside it, which is then controlled via an external remote or by the lighting desk, that projects flames out of it. There is an example of this on the website. The duration of the flames on these types of machines are dependent on the gas or fluid that they use. The Salamander is a single cartridge flame projector and can run for approximately 12 seconds without stopping, or around 30 very short bursts of around half a second each. 12 seconds might not seem a lot, but they generate a lot of heat as you would expect, and the longer they are on for, the higher they project. It is probable that you wouldn't run them for more than a few seconds at a time. You can get multi-canister machines that last a lot longer.

As with everything you do on stage, health and safety plays a huge part. Note that to have pyrotechnics in your show, first off you will have to get permission from the venue, then you will have to have someone who is trained, or at least has a good understanding of the operation of the devices as they can be harmful and potentially fatal if used incorrectly.

The person who is operating the pyrotechnics has to have a full, unobstructed view of the area of the stage where the pyros are set and it is their call as to if the pyro is set off or not. There is a minimum required distance between a person and the pyro, this distance is set by the manufacturer of the particular pyrotechnic that you are using, but it is usually around 2 metres for both performer and audience members. If there is a performer closer than that to the pyro, the person responsible for firing them must not set it off.

It is probable that if using pyros of any type, the venue will insist on a risk assessment from you. In fact, regardless of if you're using pyros or not, the venue may still insist on a risk assessment when they take your booking. There is an example of a risk assessment later in the book and an editable template available in the downloads section of the website.

If using pyros, make sure that everyone who is on stage at the time of the pyro going off has at least seen a test fire of it. You shouldn't leave it to the first performance to let them off for the first time.

When calculating how many of the pyros you need for the duration of your run, take into account rehearsal runs and test fires.

In addition to pyrotechnic and flame effects, you can also get confetti cannons and streamer cannons, which are similar to pyros, but contain confetti or streaming string, a bit like large party poppers.

There are many other special effects you can use in your performance, usually just restricted by your imagination, your time, and more importantly, your budget.

A few years ago, I did a dance show where there was a section based on the story of The Snow Queen. The set mainly consisted of high rise steel deck staging, video projection and long lengths of material hanging off one of the flying bars, but towards the end of the picce, it started to snow, light at first, but getting heavier and heavier, filling the stage with (fake) snow, then at the end, we pulled out a large industrial fan which created a snow storm on stage and in the auditorium.

I have to admit, we got this idea from a section of a Cirque Du Soleil show I had seen, which was also used in a show called, The Slava Snow Show.

We used white flutter fetti, which you can buy quite cheaply online in many different colours and it comes in bags of small, rectangular tissue paper like pieces (that you need to separate and it takes ages and is incredibly tedious) that when released from above, floats slowly down. In addition to this, we also used some stage snow, which is smaller, white light weight pieces for use with theatre snow machine effects. These can all be easily sourced online.

We started off the section by using a snow machine that we had hired from a local theatre supplies company. This is rigged on one of the flying bars and is a long, thin like tray with holes in the bottom, filled with the stage snow. It has a controllable revolving arm in the middle that sort of distributes the snow evenly and slowly when activated by the lighting desk to create a lovely snow fall.

To create the next snowing effect, the fly person had rigged a large sheet onto two of the flying bars and we filled the sheet with both the flutter fetti and the stage snow. This sheet had slits cut out of it and when the fly person pulled the rope for one of the bars up and down, the flutter fetti and snow fell through the slits slowly down to the stage. This happened over a number of minutes towards the end of the routine.

At the end of the piece where the industrial fan was brought out during a black out, we used a drop box full of the flutter fetti and stage snow, and released it in front and above the fan. A drop box is just a long wooden box, usually with a hinged bottom and a small pulley block and string attached. The flutter fetti and stage snow was put inside it before the show and when you pull on the string, it pulls out a pin in the bottom of the box, to release it's content, in this case, fake snow all over the stage. The fan was turned on at the same time and the blizzard happened and looked pretty stunning. Check out the video on the website to see the clip.

The industrial fan was hired from a local building and factory supplies company, but it wasn't that expensive. The snow was also fairly cheap too, so all in all it didn't cost that much to create that effect, although we were responsible for cleaning it up every night. The snow was still knocking around the venue months later.

Flying is another great way to make your scene look spectacular, although can be pretty expensive. I did a dance production show recently where 2 of the characters were flying during certain numbers. There are a number of companies in the UK who specialise in flying for theatre. We used, 'Flying by Foy' who deal with many of the largest shows in the West End, including Harry Potter. When using flying, there are generally a number of options, depending on what you want and what your budget is. The cheapest way is by using a single wire with just an up and down option. This can be both manually operated by someone pulling a rope, or it can be automated with a motor which has been preprogrammed. You can also have a double wire, which is what we had and the option of not only going up and down, but side to side too. Regardless of which option you choose, almost certainly the company providing the facilities will have to come and set it up for you and then train an operator for the shows. Only the person they train is allowed to operate.

With bigger venues and bigger budgets, you could think about using water effects, such as rain curtains. This is basically a pipe rigged above the stage with holes in it and water is pumped through, creating a rain effect. Although it can look stunning, this isn't really realistic in most venues as not only do you need to think of the cost and the time to rig it and make it work, but you need to think about the drainage of the water on the stage, which is quite a big task. It can look great though if time and budget allows.

PROPS

Props is a shortened version of the word, 'properties'. A prop is something, usually portable, that a performer uses on stage that isn't part of the actual set. This could be anything from a walking stick, (for the comedy Charlie Chaplin routine) to a suitcase (for the leaving to make it big routine).

It is often something that is personal to the performer's part or character – a, 'personal property', and the performer is often responsible for collecting and returning their own props.

During the performance, props (which aren't too big) are kept on a, 'Props Table'. This is exactly what it sounds like, it's a table that you use to keep the props on.

The way in which it differs to just a normal table is, the top of the table is usually split into sections with tape and then clearly labelled.

PVC electrical tape or white Gaffa Tape is commonly used to create the partitions. These are available from most electrical or housing stores, B&Q, Homebase etc.

Before the performance, it is important that someone is responsible for checking that all of the props needed for the show are on the props table, in the correct place (or next to it if too large). This could be the job of the Stage Manager or even the job of the performer, Once the table has been set, NOBODY touches anything on it, apart from the performer, who at the time comes to collect their prop.

Do not allow anyone to come and play or mess about with the props, as it is important that you know where they are at all times, so time isn't wasted when the performer comes to collect them.

One thing to think about though when using props, especially large props is, 'do you actually need it?'. The reason I mention this is, you may be using something like a large chest, or benches for your routine. This may be fine in your performance venue, but if you're performing the routine in competitions or festivals, remember that you have to get them there.

I was involved in having to get some rather large props to Spain for the Dance World Cup. We ended up paying somebody to drive them over there and then we had to get a taxi to where they were staying to pick them up. In hindsight, maybe something smaller could have been used.

STAGE GEOGRAPHY

Theatre has it's own terms for all areas of the stage (and off stage). These terms are universal but can cause a bit of confusion if you're not aware of them. Below is a list of terms and where they relate to. We will take it in stages (no pun intended) to make it easier.

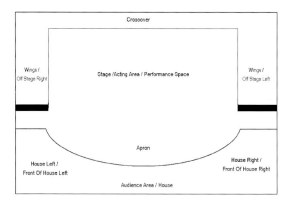

Stage Geography Part 1

The Stage / Acting Area / Performance Space - This is fairly self-explanatory, and is the area in view of the audience where the performance takes place.

Off Stage Right - This area is still on the actual stage, but is the part that the audience can't see. From the perspective of standing on the stage looking towards the audience, this is to the right-hand side.

Off Stage Left - This area is still on the actual stage, but is the part that the audience can't see. From the perspective of standing on the stage looking towards the audience, this is to the left-hand side.

Wings - Wings is the term given to the areas on both sides of the stage that the audience can't see. The term wings is generic to both sides.

Crossover - This is the area, sometimes part of the actual stage itself, or usually a back corridor running parallel to the stage where a performer can get from one side of the stage to the other out of view to the audience.

Apron - This is the part of the stage, forward of the proscenium arch (see earlier chapter). It's the area where there is often an orchestra pit. If there is no orchestra pit and the stage continues on the same level, this is known as the apron.

Audience Area / House / Front of House - This is the area of the auditorium where the audience are. It is often referred to as, 'The House', and also, 'Front of House', although, technical, Front of House is the part of the venue outside of the auditorium, such as the bar, box office, reception etc.

House Left / Front of House Left - This is the left-hand side of the auditorium from a perspective of facing the stage.

House Right / Front of House Right - This is the right-hand side of the auditorium from a perspective of facing the stage.

PART 2

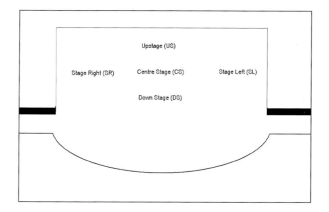

Stage Geography Part 2

Note that all of these terms are from the performer's perspective, looking towards the audience.

Stage Right - This is the right half of the stage (from centre) when you're facing the audience. If you're moving, 'stage right', the audience see you moving to their left. When written down, it is simply abbreviated to, 'SR'.

Stage Left - This is the left half of the stage (from centre) when you're facing the audience. If your moving, 'stage left', the audience see you moving to their right. When written down, it is simply abbreviated to, 'SL'.

Upstage - This is the area towards the back of the stage when facing the audience. So if you're walking towards the back wall of the stage, you are walking upstage. When written down, it is simply abbreviated to, 'US'. It is known as, upstage, because years ago, many stages had a slight incline towards the back, so you would travel up the stage to get to the back wall.

Downstage - This is the area towards the front of the stage when facing the audience. So, if you're walking towards the audience, you are walking downstage. When written down, it is simply abbreviated to, 'DS'.

PART 3

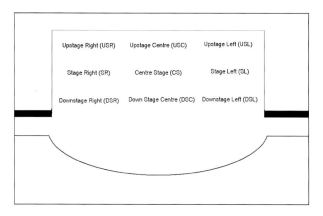

Stage Geography Part 3

We have learnt the basic stage geography terms, we will know go a bit in depth and fill in the gaps. Again, all terms are from the performer's perspective, looking into the audience.

Upstage Right - This is the area towards the back of the stage (upstage) and stage right. When written down, it is simply abbreviated to, 'USR'.

Stage Right - This is the right half of the stage (from centre) when you're facing the audience. If you're moving, 'stage right', the audience see you moving to their left. When written down, it is simply abbreviated to, 'SR'.

Downstage Right - This is the area towards the front of the stage (down stage) and stage right. When written down, it is simply abbreviated to, 'DSR'.

Upstage Centre - This is the upstage part of the centre of the stage. When written down, it is simply abbreviated to, 'USC'.

Centre Stage - This is just exactly as it says, it's just the centre area of the stage (performance area). When written down, it is simply abbreviated to, 'CS'.

Downstage Centre - This is the downstage part of the centre of the stage. When written down, it is simply abbreviated to, 'DSC'.

Upstage Left - This is the area towards the back of the stage (upstage) and stage left. When written down, it is simply abbreviated to, 'USL'.

Stage Left - This is the left half of the stage (from centre) when you're facing the audience. If your moving, 'stage left', the audience see you moving to their right. When written down, it is simply abbreviated to, 'SL'.

Downstage Left - This is the area towards the front of the stage (down stage) and stage left. When written down, it is simply abbreviated to, 'DSL'.

PART 4

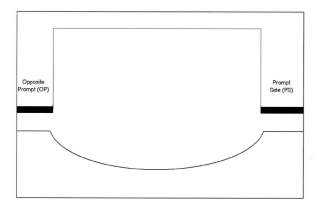

Stage Geography Part 4

We're nearly there with the stage geometry, but there are a couple more terms you may well come across.

Although the terms, stage left and stage right are most widely used, you may also hear them referred to as, 'Prompt Side' and, 'Opposite Prompt'.

Prompt Side - This refers to the area where someone, 'calls the show' (see later chapter) from, or, 'prompts' an actor who forgets their lines. In theatre world, this is traditionally the job of the, 'Deputy Stage Manager' (also referred to as, 'DSM). This is the person who is giving all of the instructions to the many different operators, lighting, sound, flys etc. That person usually will have a desk or small control station known as a, 'Prompt Desk'. The location of the prompt desk is referred to as, 'Prompt Corner'. Traditionally, prompt corner is just off stage in the downstage left corner. When this is the case, stage left is also known as, 'Prompt Side'.

Opposite Prompt - This is the opposite side of the stage to prompt side, traditionally, stage right.

If the venue's prompt corner is in the off stage, downstage right corner', this is opposite to tradition and known as, 'Bastard Prompt'.

Note - When referring to any position on the stage itself, you use the stage terminology, which is from the perspective of standing on the stage, looking into the audience - stage left, stage right, upstage, downstage etc.

When referring to anything in the auditorium, which also includes the main sound loudspeakers, you use the auditorium, or house terminology, which is from the perspective of the audience, looking to the stage - house left, house right etc.

OTHER STAGE / VENUE GEOGRAPHY TERMINOLOGY

In addition to the parts of the stage and the auditorium listed above, there are a number of other rooms / places that you will come across.

Back Stage - This is the area behind the stage, where the performers are and where the audience aren't, or at least, shouldn't be.

Front of House - As mentioned, occasionally, the auditorium, or house is referred to in some venues as, 'Front of House', but this isn't strictly true. It's the opposite of back stage, and is the public area of the venue where the public are allowed. Cafe, bar area etc. Sometimes the main loudspeakers in the auditorium are referred to as the, 'Front of House Speakers'.

Dressing Rooms - These are the rooms that are usually back stage, where the performers get changed and ready for their show.

Band Room - Sometimes, in addition to dressing rooms, some venues may have a band room / rooms. These are usually just larger dressing rooms, where traditionally members of an orchestra will get changed and prepare for their show.

Orchestra Pit - Also known as just, 'the pit', is the area traditionally where the band or orchestra are during a performance. It is usually on a lower level in front of the stage, or the stage's apron. Often the apron of a stage will actually be a lift, or set of lifts, which lower down to create an orchestra pit, which is accessed from under the stage.

Fly Floor - Also referred to as just, 'Flys', this is the area where the fly person will be to, 'fly in and out' the, 'flying bars' (see earlier section). The can be situated either off stage left or off stage right and is usually on a higher level to the stage.

Control Room - Many venues have a dedicated control room for their lighting and / or sound control position. It is also common for the control position, especially sound, to be in the actual auditorium.

Observation Box - Often shortened to, 'Obs Box', this a common room in many venues. It's a room, usually at the back of the auditorium where someone can view the production without being in the actual auditorium.

Green Room - Some venues will have a green room. This is a room where the staff and performers can relax and often able get something to eat or drink.

HOW TO CALL A SHOW

We have looked how to lay out a cue sheet and talked about how lighting and sound is controlled, but rarely should you expect the operators to be left to get on with it without any additional help. What might seem simple and obvious to you, might make no sense at all to someone who isn't familiar with the piece, so there may be occasions where you are the person in charge of, 'Calling the show'. This means you would be the person solely responsible for telling the lighting operator when to run their lighting cues, the sound operator when to start the music, the fly person when to bring a bar in or out and every other instruction to every department for that performance. This may seem really daunting, especially if you haven't done it or seen it done before, but it's actually quite straight forward once you know the logic and protocol and understand the order and terminology used. In the theatre world, this is usually the job of the Deputy Stage Manager (referred to as the DSM), or sometimes the Stage Manager (referred to as the SM).

The DSM, or whoever is calling the show, will usually have a, 'book'. This is a copy of the script which documents every cue for every department and all stage directions. It is also their job to make the backstage calls, to call the performers to the stage at the right time.

In the case of your dance show, it needn't be as complex as having a 'book' in the same way as a theatre production, but you should still provide someone to call the show for you. It could be yourself calling the show, or one of the teachers, parents or even one of the venue stage technicians, but someone usually needs to take charge, so you need the information written down in some way that can easily be understood.

Every cue for every department will have it's own exclusive cue number, which relates to their operation. The word that makes the operator go on their cue, surprisingly enough, is, 'Go'. For every cue, you will also need to give a stand by command. This is done so the relevant operator, knows that their cue is coming up soon and informs them which cue they need to perform.

The way you call a show is universal, so all theatre technicians will be expecting it to be done in this certain way.

A piece of theatre can be incredibly complex when it comes to cueing a show, but we will keep our example simple and relate it to a simple dance show.

BEFORE THE SHOW - BACKSTAGE CALLS

In the time leading up to the show starting, you will need to make a number of calls to both front of house and backstage. These are to let the company and the audience know when the show is going to begin. Most venues will deal with their own front of house calls, either with their resident stage manager, or by prerecording's.

One important thing you need to know is that all backstage calls are traditionally called five minutes earlier than they are actually for. For example, if your show is starting at 7pm, you would give a 'half hour call' to everyone backstage at 6.25 rather than 6.30, the quarter hour call would be at 6.40 rather than 6.45 etc. This is because you would give a 'Beginners' call' at 6.55, which is when everyone involved in the show's first routine, or first few routines have a few minutes to make their way to the stage from their dressing rooms, hopefully resulting in starting the show on time.

Like cueing a show, there is also a standard way of how you make your calls.

This is a list of calls you would do for backstage.

Half hour call - this happens 35 minutes before the start time of the show
Quarter hour call - this happens 20 minutes before the start time of the show
5 minute call - this happens 10 minutes before the start time of the show
Beginners Call - this happens 5 minutes before the start time of the show.

At some point, usually within the half hour leading up to the show, when the auditorium is opened to the public, you should also give the company a, '**House open**' call.

For front of house, as I mentioned, most venues will deal with this themselves with either their stage manager making the calls or they may have prerecorded calls.

If for some reason, you are faced with having to make them yourself, the calls you would do are;

House is open call - when the front of house manager is ready to let audience into the auditorium. This would go something along the lines of, "Ladies and gentlemen, the auditorium is now open for this evening's performance of (whatever the name of the show is). Please take your seats. Thank you."

5 minute call – "Ladies and gentlemen, the performance of (whatever the name of the show is) will commence in five minutes. Please take your seats. Thank you."

3 minute call - "Ladies and gentlemen, the performance of (whatever the name of the show is) will commence in three minutes. Please take your seats. Thank you."

1 minute call - "Ladies and gentlemen, the performance of (whatever the name of the show is) will commence in three minutes. Please take your seats. Thank you."

About To Begin - "Ladies and gentlemen, the performance of (whatever the name of the show is) about to begin. Please take your seats. Thank you."

Unlike the backstage calls, these do relate to the actual start times of the performance, so on a 7pm show, the 5 minute front of house call will actually be at 6.55 and so on, although sometimes, they will cheat them back a few minutes to try and get all of the audience in and help it all start on time.

For example, let's suppose your show is called, 'Get Up and Dance', the backstage calls would go like this….

House is open call – "Ladies and gentlemen of the get Up and Dance Company, the house is now open, please do not cross the stage. Thank you."

This call is done to inform the company that the audience are now starting to come into the auditorium.

The half hour call – "Ladies and gentleman of the Get Up and Dance Company, this is your half hour call, you have thirty minutes, thank you."

The quarter hour call – "Ladies and gentlemen of the Get Up and Dance Company, this is your quarter hour call, you have fifteen minutes, thank you."

The 5 minute call – "Ladies and gentlemen of the Get Up and Dance Company, this is your five minute call, you have fifteen minutes, thank you."

The beginner's call - "Ladies and gentlemen of the Get Up and Dance Company, this is your beginners call, all beginners to the stage please. Thank you."

Notice that you always say thank you at the end of your call. This is a theatre etiquette that has been handed down over time, and manners cost nothing.

CALLING THE SHOW

Depending on the venue, when all of the audience are in the auditorium, you, or one of the stage crew will receive, 'Front of House Clearance' from the Front of House Manager. The is to let you know backstage, that everyone in front of the stage is ready for the show to start and all of the audience have got into the auditorium. You should not start your show until you have been given this clearance.

Once this clearance has been given, or, in the minutes leading up to clearance, the next thing to do is, 'stand by' everybody who is involved. All of your operators will be in communication with you via their cans (headphone communications system). You need to put everyone who has a cue at the beginning of the show on to stand by. By, 'stand by', I mean that this is the command you give the operator or performer prior to actually telling them when to go on their cue. It's a way of telling people to get ready and that the cue is coming up shortly.

In this example, we'll say that in the opening section of the show requires the house lights to fade out, followed by the house tabs flying out, the, as the house tabs get half way out, the first lighting state wants to happen, followed by the music starting when the house tabs are all the way out.

Assuming front of house clearance had been given and you are happy that everyone is ready on stage, this is what you would say, but after each order, wait for the operator to respond with the words, 'Standing By', which acknowledges to you that the operator is ready.

"**Stand by house lights**" (Lighting operator replies, 'standing by' to acknowledge they are ready)

"**Stand by house tabs**" (The fly person, or whoever is controlling the house tabs replies, 'standing by')

"**Stand by LX Q1**" (The lighting operator replies, 'standing by')

"**Stand by sound Q 1**" (The sound operator replies, 'standing by')

When everyone has acknowledged that they are, 'standing by' and we're all happy, to start the procedure, we say....

"**House lights out Go**" - The lighting operator now starts to fade out the house lights over a pre-determined time. This is usually about ten seconds unless you have any other preference.

Once the house lights are out, you would say, "**House tabs Go**" - The fly person starts to fly out the tabs.

As the house tabs are half way out, you would say, "**LX Q1 Go**" - The lighting operator then runs the first lighting cue.

When you are ready for the music to start, you say, "**Sound Q1 Go**" - The sound operator now starts the first piece of music.

It's very important that you always give everyone who is about to do a cue a stand by command. It is also very important to say the cue in the correct order, with the type of cue (be it lighting or sound etc.) first, followed by the cue number, then finally, the 'Go' command.

The Go command is always on the point where you want the cue to be triggered. Don't wait for that point to happen then say the line, as there will be a pause until you say the word Go.

Also realise that operators are finely tuned to pushing a button on the word Go, so if you didn't call it in the right order and you said something like, Go Sound Q1, everyone who was on standby at that point would be wanting to push their button as soon as you say Go, but no one would know who it related to because you said it before you had said who the command was for. It might seem complicated, but it really is very easy.

There are no rules as to how far in advance you would give a stand by command, but I would recommend around 15 - 20 seconds or so before you give the line to run the cue. This gives everyone plenty of warning that a cue is about to come up and gives you enough time not to rush your words.

So, getting back to our example, if maybe the dancers all come to centre as part of the choreography, and you had got a lighting state prepared for that moment….

Around 15 - 20 seconds or so before the dancers get into that position, you would say,

"**Stand by LX Q2**" - make sure the operator responds by saying Standing by

Just as the dancers are getting into the position you want the lighting cue to happen on, start to say, "**LX Q2….**", then at the exact moment you want the cue to be triggered, you say, "**Go**".

Always try and preempt each cue rather than starting to say the command line at the point you actually want it to happen. With a little practice, is will become very familiar.

If for example, there is a moment where a lighting cue and a sound cue have to happen at the same time, let's say, LX Q3 and Sound Q2 for example, rather than say each command line individually, like, LX Q3 Go, Sound Q2 Go, you can shorten it by saying, "**LX Q3 and Sound Q2….Go**". Both operators will go on the word Go.

If there is a fly cue, you would say, "**Stand by Fly Cue….**" whatever the number happens to be, let's say 1, then just as with the lighting and the sound, just prior to you wanting it to happen, you start the sentence, "**Fly Cue 1….**" and at the appropriate time, say, "**Go**". It is really easy and straight forward, but it is very important that you say the commands in the right order.

If it's a dance routine with a few cues within it, you could always give the stand by commands for all of the cues in that routine at the beginning of the number, so example, if there were 5 lighting cues in the routine, you could just say "**Stand by LX cues 1 – 5**". You just continue in this manner for the rest of the show.

When you get to the end of the first half or the end of the show, you need to make sure you add the cues for the house tabs (if you're using them at the end) and the house lights up too, but it is called in exactly the same was at the lighting and sound cues. For example, "**Stand by house tabs**", "**House tabs…Go**" etc.

Here, we have a copy of the cue sheet from the opening number of a show I was involved in.

Unlike theatre, where there is standard way of writing out your, 'book', there isn't really a standard way for dance, this is just a way that worked for the caller.

Reading this on it's own, out of context probably doesn't mean an awful lot, but if you go to the video section of the website, there is a video of this routine with a recording of the show being cued over the top. See if you can follow what's going on. You can download this cue sheet from the website.

THE DREAM CUE SHEET

OPENING / ENTER SANDMAN

LX 9 - PRE SHOW STATE

LX 10 - LOSE HOUSE LIGHTS AND SOUND OUT

LX 11 - AS MADDY WALKS TO THE MUSIC BOX

LX 12 - "TWINKLE' (3RD TIME)

LX 13 - ON THE CHORD OF 'TWINKLE' - SHE GOES TO SLEEP AND VIDEO CHANGES

LX 14 - AS DUNCAN APPEARS FROM UNDER THE BED

LX 15 - ON "QUANG 1" - 1ST LIGHTING BUILD

LX 16 - AS THE DRUMS KICK IN

LX 17 - AS THE MAIN GUITAR RIFF STARTS

LX 21 - SALAMANDER FIRE ON BIG NOTE AT START OF MUSIC BUILD

LX 22 - AUTO FOLLOW ON FROM LX 21 - DON'T CALL

LX 23 - AS VOCAL STARTS

LX 25 - SALAMANDER FIRE ON CHORUS

LX 26 - AUTO FOLLOW ON FROM LX 25 - DON'T CALL

LX 27 - TOP OF DANCE BREAK

LX 30 - TOP OF THE LORD'S PRAYER

LX 32 - TOP OF THE NEXT CHORUS

LX 34 - SALAMANDER FIRE - ON THE WORD "BOO'

SANDMAN TRANCE

LX 35 - ON THE SITAR CHORD

LX 36 - AS MADDY GOES CENTRE STAGE

LX 37 - AS THEY MOVE TO THE BED

Example of a cue sheet for dance.

Sometimes the information includes what the lighting change is, other times, it's just the point at which the cue is given.

You will notice from the video that the lighting state is often cued a beat or so early. This is to allow the lighting operator to hear the word, 'Go' and the time it takes to hit the button on the desk. The more a show caller works with a certain lighting operator, the more it becomes second nature, and they can almost predict how long it will take them to press the Go button on the desk.

Notice that the numbers of the cues don't start at 1 and don't all go up in 1's. The reason for this is, due to the way you program a lighting desk, many programmers like to leave gaps between memory states / cues in case they want to go back and insert another state within the number.

You can also see that there are some cues highlighted. In this case, this was because these were the cues that operated the 'Salamander' fire projectors, so it was just a way of noting that extra care had to be taken when giving these cues, and a reminder to look at the stage to make sure no one was too close to the fire effects.

COPYRIGHT - PPL / PRS

As mentioned in a previous section, if ever you use any image, or recording, or song that someone else has created or written, somewhere along the line it will need to be paid for.

In the UK, and many other countries in the world, copyright in compositions is generally controlled by PRS for Music Ltd (PRS). Copyright in recordings is mostly controlled by Phonographic Performance Ltd (PPL). Both of these organisations issue licenses permitting the use of the music / recordings and charge fees for those licences, although in 2018, the two companies joined forces to create PPL PRS Ltd, to make the whole licensing process a lot easier. The money raised through those licence fees is then filtered back to the relevant composers and record companies.

It may seem a little complicated, but the PRS has a very good website which explains it all in more detail. There's a really good guide about music in performance, which I've included a link to in the downloads section of the web site.

The first thing I would suggest if that when you contact the venue with regards to putting on your show, just check with them to see if they are registered with the PRS and if they are responsible for submitting the relevant paperwork. If so, they will give you a form to fill out, where you will need to provide as much detail as possible, such as song title, composer, publisher, length of track etc. Don't be intimidated by the form, just fill out as much as you can. If the venue is not responsible for submitting the application, then it will be down to you to deal with it. You will need to visit the PRS For Music website at

https://www.prsformusic.com/licences/live-performances where you will find the download link to the, 'Variety Programme Form' to the form you will need to fill out. I have also included the form in the download section of the website.

There are a number of different categories that different types of show or different uses of music fall into, but the one which you will most likely be dealing with is the, 'V' tariff, which is the tariff that applies to variety shows at theatres and premises where admission is charged. This does not include concerts, but shows that have musical and non-musical elements such as a comedy show, dance show or pantomime. The charge is based on a percentage of receipts taken for the event and is currently 2%.

It is possible that you may be eligible to a discount, depending of the length of time that music is featured in the performance compared to the total length of the show. If the total length of music used within the show is within 25% of the total running time of the show, then you will be eligible to a 75% discount, making the total payable amount 0.5% of receipts, rather than the full 2%. If more than 25% but not more than 50%, you can claim a 50% discount, meaning you will only end up paying 1%, if the total length of music is over 50% but no more than 75%, then a 25% discount can be claimed, making it 1.5% of total receipts to be paid, but if it's over 75% of the total time, then there's no discount and the full 2% will need to be paid.

An application for a discount must be received by PRS for Music no later than five days after the first performance or ten days before the last performance, whichever date is earlier. Please contact varietyapplications@prsformusic.com for an application form.

One thing to be aware of is, although an overwhelming majority of PRS for Music's repertoire is licensable for this type of use, there are certain exclusions, for certain types of performances, which are noted in the guide. These are;

The dramatic use of the ABBA catalogue.
The use of Disney works published post 1949 in panto or dramatic presentations.
The live performance of works written by Jim Jacobs and Warren Casey from the musical, 'Grease'.

If you wish to include any Disney songs or songs from the musical 'Grease' in a pantomime, then permission in advance of performance must be sought from Warner/Chappell Music, and the PRS cannot guarantee that such permission will be granted.

Also note that Disney works published before 1949 are still subject to the grand right limitations, for example, the song, 'Heigh Ho' in a Snow White panto would be a grand right use and would not be PRS for Music controlled.

Be sure to have a look through the guide as it may have information more relevant to your particular production.

There is also a new website since PPL and PRS joined forces which can be found at www.pplprs.co.uk.

Note that the some of the above information was quoted directly from the PRS For Music website www.prsformusic.com

THEATRE ETIQUETTE

I wasn't 100% sure if I should include this section or not, as it seems like common sense, but after some of the shows I have worked on, I thought it would be useful to mention.

AUDIENCE

Obviously, it's not for me to tell anyone how to behave or not behave, but theatres have a certain etiquette to them. I'm not saying that you should dress up in formal wear, sip champagne and politely clap at the end, but there have been many occasions where the behavior of the parents in the auditorium, especially if their child is dancing, is not just unpleasant, but incredibly off-putting to many of the other audience around. This includes shouting out children's names during a routine - "come on Tracey!!" being bellowed out at the top of their voice, constant getting up for the toilet during the performance, often having to pass through rows of people to get out, bringing in food with noisy wrappers into the auditorium, taking photographs with a flash and many more off putting actions.

One frustrating habit that I have seen many parents do, is leave the auditorium once their child has danced. Many dance schools I have worked with have a policy that if a dancer is only in the first half of the show, the parents can't collect them until the interval.

I was at this year's Dance World Cup and certain groups of parents who had brought whistles and vuvuzelas into the audience got warnings from the organisers and venue staff to show a little respect in the auditorium.

If you have any 'problem parents', and let's face it, there's not many dance schools or studios that don't have at least one, then maybe try a simple email prior to your shows, just informing them about how they are expected to behave in the auditorium. I have included an example email in the downloads section of the website for you to either use as reference or to amend and use.

Remember that any disruptions or problems in the audience will always get back to the venue staff. You don't want to become known to the venue as a problem school.

BACKSTAGE

Although this should go without saying, you would be amazed at the state the backstage area has been left in after some dance schools have visited the theatre. Everything from litter, general untidiness, bathroom taps left running, paper towels in the sink and even lipstick kiss marks all over the walls and mirrors. I strongly advise that you're strict with your students and make sure the area is left in a similar way to how you found it.

Make sure you come armed with toilet rolls and bin bags, as regardless of how many toilet rolls the venue provides, at some point, when there are children involved, you will run out. Also, maybe not at the end of each night, but certainly at the end of the run, have someone go around the dressing rooms and backstage area to empty bins, have a general tidy and leave the bin bags in a place agreed with the venue staff.

As well as general tidiness, and again, this all sounds fairly obvious, but make sure the children don't run backstage. Theatres can be a dangerous place. Make sure there is someone to tell them to quieten down if the noise becomes too loud as often the noise can bleed through to the stage.

Finally, make sure you say thank you to all of the venue staff that help out on your production. It's also fairly common, especially if you have been in a venue for a few days, to buy the crew a case of beer, a bottle of wine, a tin of chocolates, or some token gesture. It was always the unwritten rule in theatre that on the last night of a show, after the crew had taken down the set of a visiting company and packed it in the back of a truck, the company manager would bring out a case of beer as a thank you. Sadly, for many reasons, this isn't as common anymore, but you will be amazed at how much it will be appreciated and how much fonder the crew will remember you by if you use that venue again another year.

CHILD LICENSING

Child licensing should be a fairly easy, standard procedure, but like everything else, it isn't that simple. Despite it being a government requirement, there seems to be slightly different interpretations of the rules, depending on the county you are in.

Below is a basic outline of what the licence is and why and when you may or not need one. This information is taken from various UK government websites, a lot of the information is common worldwide, but please do check with your local authority to get clarification for your area.

There are also some additional reading downloads regarding this matter in the download section of the website.

WHAT IS A CHILD PERFORMANCE LICENCE?

The Child Performance Licence is a government required document that effects children who perform in theatres, TV, paid sporting events and modelling who are under the compulsory school leaving age.

It is the responsibility of the production company responsible for the event, be it the dance school or studio, dance competition organiser, drama group, sports event organiser etc. to apply for the Child Performance Licence. Failure to do so can result in heavy fines if they use un licensed children in their event or production.

The licence is issued by the local education authority for the area of the child involved and not the area of the event if this is different.

If the production is being produced by their full-time academic school, then a licence is not required.

The purpose of the licence is to protect children by restricting the hours that a child can be present at a performance location, the actual working hours and to ensure they have the required amount of breaks to that period.

It also requires the production company to provide a suitable number of registered chaperones for the amount of children in the production (or event).

Children require a licence even if they are not being paid IF there is a paying audience watching the performance. There are only two exceptions to this rule. These are;

1: If the child / children have not taken part in any other performances for more than three days within the preceding six months and they do not require any absence from school and they are not being paid. Do note, that although exempt from needing a license in this situation, details still need to be submitted to the local council and an, 'exemption certificate' needs to be granted, which is still a physical document.

2: If the organisation responsible for the production or event have been granted an exemption by the local council to allow them to perform in amateur performances without the need to apply for a separate licence for each child. This is known as a Body of Persons Approval (often referred to as a BOPA).

A BOPA is often issued to dance schools, amateur dramatic companies, youth groups etc. These are still on the condition that the child or children are not being paid and don't require any absence from school.

The current regulations for performing children are covered by The Children and Young Person's Act 1963 and The Children Performance Regulations 1968. These acts can often be interpreted slightly differently by individual councils and have resulted in children becoming victims of a postcode lottery, with some councils offering more flexible licence arrangements than others.

For years, there were some councils who offered a six-month open licence to their children, which allowed the child to perform a certain amount of days within that six-month period, without having to apply for individual licenses for each event. This mean that the child could undertake professional work immediately and the council just had to be notified of the dates and details usually by email. However, some councils still insisted on individual licence applications requiring seven to twenty-eight days' notice to grant the licence. This often made it impossible for the required paperwork to be issued in time for the child to perform resulting in agents and producers favoring children who lived in the Open Licence areas. Most councils have stopped issuing an Open Licence and most councils can usually offer a licence within seven to fourteen days of receiving the required paperwork.

Children who have reached the end of their statutory education do not require a licence to perform.

Note that some of this information was taken directly from various Government websites.

CHAPERONES

In the eyes of the law, a parent or friend of the family can't legally be in charge of a child backstage other than their own. This is the job of a licensed chaperone and is requirement of the Child Performance Licence. A parent can still be a chaperone, but they have to apply for a licence.

It will be your responsibility to provide the required number of chaperones, the amount will depend on how many children there are in your school or studio.

As there is a cost to getting a chaperone licence, sometimes parents aren't happy to pay that, and expect the dance school to foot the bill. A common way of getting around this, is, especially if your school or studio regularly competes in dance festivals and competitions, is to have it in your policy that for every child who is chosen as a festival dancer, it is their parents' responsibility to apply for a chaperone licence. Often, the parent is so happy their child has been chosen to compete, they are more than willing to apply. By making this a policy, you will end up with a good amount of chaperones who can cover most events.

Local authorities are responsible for issuing chaperone or matron's licences, but these processes vary from county to county. The following is advised as a matter of best practice;

An enhanced level DBS check should be made.

An interview to assess the chaperone's suitability and competency for the role.

Two verifiable references.

Child protection training should be offered to new applicants and refresher training to those who are re applying.

At best practice, the local authority should share information of rejected chaperones with the DBS.

Note that some of this information was taken directly from various Government websites.

THE ROLE OF THE CHAPERONE

The chaperone has many roles to play. Here is a list of just some of them;

Most importantly, to be responsible for the health and safety and the welfare of a child or children.

To be in charge of no more than 12 children (all of whom are the same sex as the chaperone).

To make sure that changing rooms are occupied by children only. Children over the age of 5 have to be split into same sex dressing rooms.

Assist with changing / microphone fittings etc.

To ensure the child's comfort at all times.

To be aware of all medical conditions and to recognise if a child is feeling unwell or upset.

To oversee a parent / child sign in and sign out procedure.

To have knowledge and written permission of any person under the age of 16 for someone other than a parent to collect them.

To be aware of performance times.

To be in charge of first aid and accurately record and report to the child's parent of any incident.

There are many more duties of the chaperone. I have included a great guide in the downloads section of the website which covers all of this in more detail, along with some really useful templates and charts to help the chaperoning session.

RISK ASSESSMENT

There is a good chance, somewhere along the way, be it in your school or studio policy, or as a requirement from a venue, that you will have to create a risk assessment. This sounds a bit more complicated than it actually is.

A risk assessment is a document showing that within your workplace, or for your event, you have carefully thought about and documented any potential risks that anyone could be subjected to. It notes who is subject to these risks, and has a description on how to either avoid those risks and also what the procedure is if any of those risks actually happen.

A quick search online will find you many templates for risk assessments in different styles.

Here is an example of how a risk assessment related to your business might look.

I have included this in the downloads section of the website. Feel free to edit it to suit your needs for your production.

Name: Production: Date:

Risk?	Who may be harmed and how?	Actions	Actions by who
1. Parents handing over children to chaperones at stage door	Children coming into the theatre unescorted. They may get lost, and may be unsupervised.	Upon arrival, children will be escorted into the main hall. Licensed chaperones will be in attendance. The children will not be able to leave this space without a chaperone in attendance.	Teachers must ensure that all chaperones are aware of the time they are to be in the theatre, and have designated chaperones for escort duties. Teachers need to give information to parents regarding drop of place and time.
2. Fire	Children, chaperones, staff. Risk of fire brigade not knowing if anyone in building should there be a fire.	A register of each child, chaperone and staff member must be at the sign in desk by 14.00 hrs. No child, chaperone or member of staff will be allowed to enter or exit the theatre without signing in or out. These registers must be kept at the sign in desk with the designated sign in/out person, unless signing out children at the tea break, or at the end of the show in a different area.	Teachers to ensure registers are ready by 14.00 hrs, that they are legible and correct. It is the Teacher's responsibility to sign out the children in their care, at tea and end of show.
3. Hazardous environment. Fire drill	Children, chaperone, staff. Could put themselves in danger, if they do not know what to do if the fire alarm sounds.	All children, chaperones and staff must attend the safety brief, which will be held by the theatre technicians before the rehearsal. This will be in the auditorium at 14.00 hrs.	Teachers to ensure that all children, chaperones and staff are in auditorium by 14.00. Theatre staff to talk about safety in the theatre and fire procedure.
4. Moving around the theatre	Children – may get lost and put themselves in danger.	Children must be in the dressing rooms at all times during the performance unless they are going to or from the stage. When moving around the theatre chaperones must be with them at all times in the ratio 1 chaperone to 12 children maximum.	Teachers to ensure that they have enough chaperones to fulfil the moving of children around the theatre within the guidelines.
5. Unautherised persons in theatre	Children	The doorman may not allow any person or parent who is not listed on the register access to the theatre. In an emergency ie. a child is ill or hurt the producer of the show must give permission, and escort them to wherever they need to go, and remain with them during the time they are in the theatre.	Producer to ensure sign in person and Head Chaperone is aware of responsibilities, and how to contact producer in an emergency.
6. Trips and slips	Children – Risk of falling on stage.	There will be no foam, glitter, petals etc used in this performance. In case of injury there are designated first aiders within the chaperone team	Teachers to inform Head Chaperone each night who the first aiders are.
7. Comfort of children	Child dehydrated, cold, too hot, ill.	Chaperones should ensure the comfort of the children in their care and ensure they have enough to drink. Make sure they are not too hot/cold, and are not stressed by the rehearsal or show.	Teacher must have contact details of parents so they are able to contact them at earliest opportunity. Teachers must inform parent that their child needs to bring adequate drinks with them for duration of rehearsal and show.
8. Children leaving the theatre	Children getting lost, given to someone who is not their parent	All dancing schools have a designated area where they hand over the children to their parents at tea and show end. This is designed to make it as safe as possible so that all children are not going out of one door. Teachers must hand over children, and chaperones must accompany their group until all have been handed over.	Teachers must ensure that parents know where to pick up children so there is no confusion. They must sign each child out on their register.

FINAL SHOW CHECKLIST

Finally, I thought it might be useful to have a show checklist. This is just a simple list noting things to remember when you head off to the venue for your rehearsals.

I've started this off, it's up to you to edit or add to it to suit your needs. You can download it from the website.

WW AUDIO DANCE SHOW PERFORMANCE CHECK LIST

	Task
☐	All music on required formats plus back up disc / files
☐	Lighting notes for operator
☐	Sound notes including mic plans, lyric sheets etc
☐	Any equipment that you're providing
☐	All costumes
☐	Sewing and costume repair kits
☐	Printed signs for dressing room doors showing names or classes etc
☐	Registers
☐	First aid kit
☐	Incident book
☐	Ice packs
☐	Bin bags
☐	Toilet Rolls
☐	Contact details for all children
☐	All additional jobs covered
☐	All props
☐	Thank you cards / gifts if required
☐	
☐	
☐	

Example of Production Check List

ONLINE EXTRAS

Hopefully this book would have given you a bit more of an insight into putting on shows in professional venues. You will have noticed throughout the book, I have mentioned that there are a number of video examples, tutorials and also a collection of downloads, including useful guides of some of the topics we have talked about, but also various templates for you to download and use as you wish.

To access these, you need to visit www.wwaudio.co.uk

Once you have got to the home page, it will give you a number of options. You can either click on the link that is labelled, 'eBooks' and education' and follow the links to the members section, or you can go to the 'eBooks' drop-down tab at the top of the page, and if you hover you mouse over it, you will get another drop down menu called, 'members'. If you click on this link, you will be prompted for a password to continue.

The password to access the members section is **ayn2k1** (all lower case).

With the release of this book, I will be launching a Facebook group called, 'Dance Show Tech Support Group - #AYN2K'. The idea behind it is to have a place where people can ask technical based questions and hopefully either myself, or someone can give them the answers. Please join it and let's make it a great online information hub.

In addition to the tutorials, downloads and technical support, the website shows my sound effect libraries, sound art and field recording releases, as well as some personal information about my work and a full CV. It also has a section dedicated to sound editing services for choreographers and dance teachers. If you have bought the book, you are entitled to a discount of certain editing and production services should you want it. If you ever use the services, just mention that you have bought the book and you will get a 10% discount.

Thank you again for buying this book. Hopefully, it is the first in a series of guides relating to productions and technical services. Keep checking the website for regular updates and to learn of future releases.

Cheers

Wills

WWAUDIO.CO.UK

Sound Editing for Choreography

Let WW Audio edit the music for all your choreography needs

Making routines competition length
Editing and splicing
Supplying or adding sound effects to your tracks
Making endings stronger
Adding hits, accents and slams
Mix / blend multiple songs
Creating custom mixes of multiple tracks or clips
Cover up inappropriate language
Maximizing and levelling audio levels in the track

We can supply music in any format you require (advice given)

Have you finished choreographing and setting your piece, but the music is still falling flat compared to the amazing performance the dancers are giving? Everything coming across as a little unexciting? Send us your song and a video of your dance and let us create exciting hits and accents to match your choreography.

Brand New Service – Video Editing / Format Conversion

Do you have a video that needs editing? Let WW Audio do it for you. Supply us with the unedited files, let us know what you want and the edit will be custom made for you.

We also convert from one file format to another. Have you filmed a dance routine on your phone but you need to convert it to an MPEG 4 or any other format? Not a problem. Send us over the file and we will convert it for you. We can convert most types of video file, but contact us first to double check.

Great Rates – Quick Turn Around

Email wills.theatresound@googlemail.com for more information.

wwaudio.co.uk

#AYN2K

ALL YOU NEED TO KNOW

THE ULTIMATE GUIDE TO PUTTING ON A SHOW IN A PROFESSIONAL VENUE

DANCE STUDIO EDITION

First published 2018 By WW Audio

ISBN 978-1-68454-314-4

Copyright 2018 Matthew Williams

For more information, visit www.wwaudio.co.uk

#AYN2K

ALL YOU NEED TO KNOW

THE ULTIMATE GUIDE TO PUTTING ON

A SHOW IN A PROFESSIONAL VENUE

DANCE STUDIO EDITION

WRITTEN BY MATTHEW 'WILLS' WILLIAMS

WW AUDIO